ALL YOU NEED IS LOVE

All You Need Is Love

"Just imagine you're not a Beatles fan, but you find yourself grieving over the untimely death of John Lennon. Just imagine your grief is so overwhelming your life falls apart. Are you crazy or is there a deeper, stranger reason?

This was the dilemma of Jewelle St. James, a Canadian housewife and mother. And just imagine her surprise and awe when, in her search for answers, she finds the explanation in historical England.

Her journey in this life is rooted in a past life. And the emotionally wrenching yet satisfying answer that love never dies is for all our journeys into the next life."
— Sharon Jarvis, Author of *Dead Zones* and *Dark Zones*.

"Jewelle St. James' story is entirely convincing. I applaud her courage to speak out about something so deeply personal and, in addition, so deeply controversial. Whether or not you believe in her message of reincarnation, this amazing account will keep you riveted—-I couldn't put it down."
— Linda Keen, Author of *Intuition Magic*
and *Across the Universe with John Lennon*,
by Hampton Roads Publishing Company.

"Just Imagine. That's what John Lennon asked us to do. And Jewelle St. James did just that. The power of her belief in her love—imaginary or not—turned out to be stormy. She was blown off course, backwards in time. Long before Beatledom. This storm was for real, whether or not you end up agreeing that she must have been John Lennon's lover."

—Alan Twigg, Publisher/Writer, *BC Bookworld*

All You Need Is Love

JEWELLE ST. JAMES

St. James Publishing

CANADIAN CATALOGUING IN PUBLICATION DATA

St. James, Jewelle, 1953–
  All you need is love / by Jewelle St. James

ISBN 0-9732752-0-0

  1. St. James, Jewelle, 1953– 2. Reincarnation—Biography. I. Title.
PS8587.A3085A82 2003   133.9'01'35   C2003-910421-4
PR9199.3.S158A82 2003

Published by
St. James Publishing
P.O. Box 990
Revelstoke, B.C., VOE 2S0
Canada

Edited by David F. Rooney

Cover design by Vincent Wright

Typeset by the Vancouver Desktop Publishing Centre Ltd.

Printed and bound in Canada

Acknowledgements

Thank you to:

Sharon Jarvis, my literary agent, for your words of wisdom, encouragement, and sound advice.

Konni Frazier, my sister and friend.

Dayle Sheridan, my spiritual teacher.

Jan Tober, my earth angel.

Ros Staker, John Staker, Ann Boxall, and Tony Boxall for your love and friendship.

Peter Jerrome MBE, Marian Jerrome, Ann Bradley, Anne Simmons, Miles Costello, and the *Petworth Society* for your support.

Cindy Powell, a beacon of light on my path.

Kristy D, a dear friend, for keeping the faith.

Bob and Joan Eley, for believing in this story, and taking it world-wide.

Linda Keen, a kindred spirit.

Jason Leen, whose work with John Lennon, in spirit, is admirable.

Ron Beraducci, Tom and Sheila Cope, Dale Davis, Ron Lind, and Gordon Olsson for sharing your fond memories of Patrick White.

Past life regressonists and psychics extraordinaire: Laara Bracken, Therese Dorer, Angela Filippelli, Loren Greig, Dane Purschke, Victoria Moria Simmonds, Petula Stowell, Dan Valkos, Becky Webber, Cecilia Wilkinson, and Sophie Young.

My family: Mom, Dad, Angelo, Belinda, Brenda, Desmond, Destiny, Gage, Harvie, Jayden, Jeff, Jewelle, Joanne, Korinn, Kristy, Larry, Margaret, Martin, Michael, Norm, Peter, Ryan, and Shane. And Kane.

Patrick White for guiding me, with love, from above.

Patty Osborne for your expertise, and patiently answering my endless questions. Thanks Patty!

Ingrid Nelson and Diane Ganten for contributing, each uniquely, to my manuscript.

Raffaele Pasceri for your professionalism, assisting me, in completing the manuscript.

Vincent Wright for your artistic genius, creating this beautiful book cover.

David F. Rooney for superb editing.

Those in the cheering section!

Mieke Blommestein, Mary Carlson, Sonia Cinelli, Dick Earl, Allison Elmes, Paulette Gaudreault, Joan Holzer, Barb Kalinczuk, Barb Kemerer, Janine Kohlman, Vicki Kushner, Kathy Lingren, Frida Livesey, Doug May, Eleanora McKenzie, Rosalyn Nelles, Bev Odorizzi, Norma Olynyk, Yonda Oostenhoff, Lloyd Oram, Janet Pearson, Kelly Richards, Ria Groenedijk Van Rossum, Lisa Schwartzenhauer, Sheila Stephenson, Al Tennant, Mary Thompson, Sydney Thompson, Coreen Tucker, Jaime Walker, Christie Wassing, Sara Watson, Myra Wendy, Zella Wohrmann, June Wood, and Herma Worman.

The readers of *Just Imagine*, and Eric H, who encouraged me to continue writing.

Permission granted from the *Fraser Valley Record*, Mission, B.C. for reproduction of the editorial on John Lennon.

Permission granted from the *Midhurst and Petworth Observer*, Chichester, West Sussex for reproduction of articles.

Author's Note

All You Need Is Love encompasses, and is the continuation of my earlier book, *Just Imagine*.

Another name change is my (previous) surname, Lewis, to my present surname, St. James.

In October, 2001, I received a channeled explanation of the drive, often consuming me, to discover my own truth.

This message was delivered through a delightful lady, Myra Wendy, from her spirit guide, on a beautiful afternoon in the Sussex countryside.

In this life, Jewelle is a wanderer after truth . . . there is a great seeking and a need to know; this is a mission and it must be complete before her life can depart and reunite . . . the energies are strong and forceful and Jewelle is carried along with them . . . all else has to cease . . . she is guided and cannot deviate from this task. We work with love, love is powerful without fear . . . love is the most powerful force; whatever fear does . . . love will eventually surface and heal.

Dear Reader

I thank you for accompanying me on this journey. Your presence, I value.

Jewelle St. James
June, 2003

For John

One

"So you think you've lived a past life with John Lennon?" my husband, Bob, would ask. Sensible, level-headed Bob.

I would answer his questions with my usual question, "Well, can you explain all of this?"

I always hoped he could explain because I certainly couldn't. I hoped someone, anyone, could explain.

But a past life with John Lennon? I'll let you be the judge.

It all started December 9, 1980, the day after John Lennon was shot.

The stillness of that early morning was interrupted only by the irregular sound of perking coffee. I always savored those quiet moments before the flurry of getting kids ready for school.

Unbeknownst to me, my simple ordinary life, as a young wife and mother, would change (forever) in the next few seconds.

I recall flipping on the radio and as *White Christmas* played softly, I stood at the kitchen window and watched the lightly falling snow. I was once again caught up in the anticipation of the approaching Christmas season. With the end of the Irving Berlin melody, the news announcer broke into the Yuletide mood with the 7:00 a.m. news.

"John Lennon was fatally shot last evening in New York City just before 11 o'clock. Lennon's wife, Yoko Ono, was with him at the time of the shooting, which occurred just outside their home at the Dakota Apartments. Mark David Chapman, who claimed to be a fan of the ex-Beatle, is being held in custody and has been charged with the shooting. No further details are known at this time."

I recall thinking, 'John Lennon . . . New York . . . so that's where you've been.' New York; a different planet than my world in a small mountainous Canadian town. *Revelstoke, British Columbia; gateway to the Rocky Mountains;* a tourist ad might say. My head spun as I mechanically got my children off to school.

Images of my own childhood flashed before me. My summer friend, Daphne, and me sitting on a North Shuswap Lake beach, one hot August afternoon in 1964, planning a trip to Vancouver to see the Beatles. I was only eleven years old; the great disappointment of not being able to go soon forgotten amidst the other activities of that summer. Only now, years later, I found myself thinking about it.

My thoughts were erratic. 'New York . . . why didn't I find that out . . . before it was too late? Why haven't I been paying attention to where he has been?' Inexplicable feelings of grief, desperation, and loss washed over me leaving me drained and confused.

The radio stations played a mixture of Christmas carols and Beatles' music. It had been so long since I had heard the Beatles' hits and most of John Lennon's music was new to me.

Later, I huddled at the end of the sofa, hugging my knees and staring into space. John Lennon's *In My Life* filled the room. An ache penetrated my being so deeply that I thought I would die. Tears slid down my cheeks. My mind went numb. While the radio continued to send out its musical tributes to the slain John Lennon, I wept, and time stood still. My sobbing eventually subsided and I drifted off to sleep.

I was vaguely aware of Bob entering the foyer, brushing the snow from his hair. The only noise came from the radio. I heard him turn it off. Bob's warm hand was on my cheek and his voice expressed concern. "You okay?"

I blurted, "John Lennon was shot!"

He nodded. "Yeah, I heard."

I tried to explain. "I just feel so sad. I haven't thought of the Beatles since I was a kid and I guess it brought back some memories of when I was young or something . . . I don't know." I was feeling self-conscious. "I really don't know why it has hit me this way."

Suddenly, the children burst in through the double doors, laughing and fighting at the same time. Flinging coats and snow-covered mittens about, they ran to the kitchen emerging with mouths and hands full of cookies.

Bob suggested that we get our Christmas tree before the snow was too thick to see anything. I agreed, not wanting to admit that I hadn't noticed the unusually heavy snowfall. As the kids piled noisily into the car, I couldn't help getting caught up in their excitement as we set out to find the perfect tree.

Driving through the streets it was easy to see the evidence of the day's snowfall. The fresh heavy snow smothered everything, creating a story-book effect. As we did every Christmas, we left the Trans-Canada highway and headed towards the back woods.

Bob became a lumberjack for the time it took to find the perfect tree. Critically, he eyed tree after tree, knocking the heavy snow off each, to make just the right choice. The children screeched with delight as each tree shed its billowing, snowy shower. With nightfall quickly approaching, they were content to begin the journey home with the promise of hot chocolate awaiting. I felt safe and warm as we sped through the night, the branches of our tree bouncing and brushing rhythmically against the car's roof and windows. The interior was filled with the sweet aroma of spruce from the resin on the warm mitts and jackets.

Bob switched on the car radio and we drove through the snowy night accompanied by the strains of *Silent Night*.

Then, unannounced, John Lennon's haunting voice filled the car with *Starting Over*, and I had to stare fixedly out the window into the darkness so Bob wouldn't notice my sudden tears.

Two days later, my grief seemed to have subsided. I was aware of Bob watching me as I seemed absorbed in Christmas preparations. Actually, I was chastising myself for wasting those precious days before Christmas, grieving for a rock star I hadn't thought about for over fifteen years.

'Dammit, what's the matter with me? He was a rock star . . . not part of my world. Get your act together!'

The next morning I felt my usual self. Minutes after the children had devoured stacks of pancakes and left for school, I wrapped a Christmas parcel and felt glad that everything was back to normal. I drove to the nearby shopping mall, light-heartedly making a mental list of Christmas chores that needed attention.

At the mall, my first stop was at a small postal counter in the drug store. As I waited my turn in line, I heard John Lennon's *Woman* being played on the store's sound system. Suddenly I felt ill. The clerk took my parcel and placed it on the scale, pushing the weights this way and that. I had to escape the music.

Angry and nauseated, I grabbed the parcel, snapping at the

clerk, "Oh, forget it! I'll take it to the main post office where they know what they are doing."

Not caring that people were staring at me, I bolted for the door, jumped in my car, and headed downtown. *Woman* pursued me from the car radio that I didn't think to silence. Oblivious to the tears streaming down my face, I wove in and out of traffic. Suddenly there were two elderly women on a crosswalk in front of me. I slammed on the brakes; the car slid for endless seconds on an icy patch. The two women, laughing and chattering, walked on, totally unaware of me.

From inside my closed car, I screamed at them and the world, "Why are you so happy? Don't you care that John Lennon is dead?" Shaken, I sat for a moment until, from behind me, the blare of a car's honking horn brought me back to my senses. As I moved again with the flow of traffic, I resolved to get myself together.

Two

I was still shaking as I reached the end of our long driveway, and found sanctuary in my kitchen. I was just beginning to relax with a steaming cup of tea when the telephone rang. It was an old friend inviting herself over for a visit. Mechanically I agreed; but not really wanting company that afternoon.

Unintentionally, I lapsed into a reverie about a period of my life, ten years earlier, when I met Debbie.

Just days after my sixteenth birthday, scared as hell, I enrolled in Revelstoke Secondary School. I had never seen a school so enormous, nor had I ever been the new kid at school. At my home high school (to quote my mom), I had exhibited more interest in partying than studying and had started running around with the wrong crowd. Finally, my parents had had enough and sent me to live with an aunt. To be allowed back home I would have to change my ways. The school counsellor assigned Debbie to introduce me around the school; show me the ropes. I was so relieved to have her help that I didn't complain that she didn't seem to be my type.

Debbie was plump, wore her hair long and straight, and projected an air of know-it-all superiority. Being in charge of the "new girl" swelled her sense of self-importance. Smiling at everyone, Debbie took great pains to fill me in on the backgrounds of most students; I was amused and entertained by Debbie's analysis of her classmates. I soon learned her opinion of who was worth knowing and who wasn't; who were partiers; who wore their skirts too short, or their hair too long.

One day, as we filled in time between classes, a tall, muscular boy with warm blue eyes strolled along the hallway in our direction. When he spotted me, he widened his eyes and mockingly gave me an exaggerated grin. I turned to watch after he passed only to see him walking backwards, still smiling at me.

I burst out laughing and asked Debbie, "Who was that?"

Debbie was very serious in her reply, saying his name was Patrick White, that he was crazy, and that I should stay away from him. In the meantime I was thinking that maybe Revelstoke Secondary School wouldn't be so bad after all.

To my disappointment Patrick only occasionally attended school, and when I questioned Debbie about how he got away with skipping so many days, she testily replied that he got straight As, and that the principal likely felt that anyone who could do that by coming to school once a week deserved to come and go as he pleased.

One day, as Debbie and I were leaving school, a motorcycle roared through the parking lot, weaving its noisy path through parked cars and screeched to a stop beside us. To my delight, when the cyclist removed his helmet, there was Patrick and he was asking me to go for a spin. Without hesitating I clambered on behind him, he buckled the helmet on my head, and accelerated away so quickly my eyes watered. Strangely, as I clung to his leather jacket, I felt protected by this spirited young man, who would, in later years, be the father of my first child. I lost my son through adoption and later I lost Patrick through death.

Forcing myself back to the present, I dialed Debbie's number. I abruptly gave her the excuse that I was not feeling well, and promised to meet on another day.

Later that evening, I took a hot bubbly bath accompanied by my newspaper. As I lay back in anticipation of welcome relaxation, I spotted the headline, *John Lennon: Was He Really So Great?*

Jewelle, December, 1980. Days after the death of John Lennon.

Three

The article that caught my attention accompanied the announcement that a traveling evangelist preacher, the Reverend Tom Allen, was to speak on the topic, *John Lennon: Was He Really So Great?* My eyes quickly scanned the article and I couldn't believe some of the Reverend's opinions.

Lennon and the Beatles, through their music, were responsible for promoting such modern maladies as sexual immorality, drug addiction, revolutionary politics, and Eastern religions.

The mood and theme of those years of Beatlemania were simple: sex. With songs Love Me Do, Please Please Me, and She Loves You, these four men set an immoral course for North America.

How can a man live his life promoting sexual immorality, revolutionary politics, and Eastern religions, only to be hailed as a hero when he dies?

Certainly his violent death can be connected with the judgment of God. Lennon lived his entire life in rejection of authority figures and was shot to death by a young man who had no respect for authority figures either.

This very day there is no heaven for John Lennon. He has gone to meet his Creator.

John Lennon will meet eternal death in a place called Hell.
There will be more, of course, on Sunday, when the topic will
be, "Rock and Roll, the Bible and the Mind."

I was furious. I jumped out of the tub, splashing water everywhere. Drying quickly, and throwing on a bathrobe, I flew to the kitchen to collect paper and pen. I switched on the lamp, sat at my end of the sofa, and began to write.

Dear Mr. Editor:

Never has a newspaper article infuriated me as (did) yours on the late John Lennon. Proclaiming that Lennon will face eternal death in Hell and that his violent death was connected to God's judgment . . . does this also apply to Martin Luther King, John Kennedy, and other victims of violence?

John Lennon was an advocate of peace and love, which we needed in the 60s and need today even more. The Beatles' early music, through to John's last works, told of love, not sexual immorality. We cried when John Lennon died because part of us died too. The Beatles taught us there were alternatives to the ideas of former generations, and that we could live in peace and harmony with one another. The rest was up to us.

So, please don't use your newspaper to allow others to slander him in the name of God.

Without missing a beat I recopied my outburst, hastily folded the single sheet of paper, and slipped it into an envelope.

I was back on my favorite couch, staring unseeingly, when it dawned on me that I had never written a letter to a newspaper before; the very thought of publicly expressing an opinion had always paralyzed me. Oddly, I was doing so now without hesitation.

Four

The Christmas season was over; the radio's odd mixture of traditional carols and Beatles' music vacated the airwaves; television networks had exhausted their documentaries on John Lennon, and magazine covers no longer bore the famous faces of the *Fab Four*. 1980 had passed into history, taking with it the sensationalism of Lennon's death.

At the usual time one morning the telephone rang. Expecting Debbie home after a Christmas visit to the Okanagan, I quickly poured a cup of coffee, and answered the phone. Not wasting a moment, and with an almost accusing tone in her voice, Debbie told me how she had spotted my letter in the local newspaper.

"Since when do you write letters to the editor . . . since when do you care so much about music . . . and since when do you defend people like *John Lennon?*"

When I wrote the letter I really hadn't thought of the reaction it might provoke in the people I knew. I couldn't think of why it would be a big deal. I tried to explain to Debbie that I wasn't defending John Lennon's music, only Lennon himself.

"But why does it matter that I wrote a letter?" I asked.

"That's what I'd like to know, Jewelle! Why did it matter

enough to you that you would write a letter to the paper? I mean he was just a long-haired . . . and those silly glasses . . ."

I laughed her off. I humored her, saying I thought John Lennon was cute. That didn't satisfy her and she hung up in a huff. Oh well, I thought, she was always opinionated.

Weeks passed; the world seemed to forget the loss of a great human being. Little did I realize John Lennon's music and philosophies would live on.

For the next three years I quietly hid an unbearable, cold, empty ache. I lived two lives; one as mother and wife, and the other as a compulsive collector of Beatles' and John Lennon's music and trivia.

One dreary April afternoon in 1984, I snapped. I had to reach out to someone; but to whom? I would write to Yoko! I bought expensive stationary, a fine pen, and had written, *Dear Yoko*, before I realized how ridiculous the whole idea was. I felt humiliated. What in hell was I doing? Had I really lost it, become a lovesick fan? One day I knew I would have to turn to someone, but Yoko Ono was not that someone.

Later that wet spring day, I made a purchase that was to be the first step toward understanding. After finishing my shopping, I found myself sidetracked to a record store, emerging with a copy of the *Imagine* album. Having never heard it before, I played the record as soon as I got home. Curled up on the sofa, watching the rain driving against the window, I really heard Lennon's songs for the first time. It was when the track of *Jealous Guy* began that I experienced a vivid recollection of an ancient milestone nestled in rich green grass at the edge of a narrow roadway. Still legible in the darkened granite were the words, ". . . miles to London." It was the same image that came to my mind's eye when, as a child in school, I listened to the teacher read the old English story, *Dick Whittington's Cat*.

Why was that image evoked by that song? Why had I seen

this exact image twice and so clearly? Plausible explanations eluded me, but I knew there was someone I could ask, and it was finally time to do just that. I picked up the telephone and dialed my mother's number in Vancouver.

"Grandma's here! Grandma's here!" heralded Mother's arrival the next day. She distributed hugs all around before shedding her coat, whereupon the children pulled her into their rooms where she was bombarded with school projects, stories, and all the important things in their lives.

The daughter of a lumberjack, my mother had left her parents' rural home on the North Shuswap Lake during World War II. Times were hard for her parents, who had five other children to provide for. Moving to Kamloops, she boarded with strangers and worked for her room and board while attending high school. She later became a certified teacher. This experience developed her strong will and lifelong self-reliance.

My father was attracted to this confident woman who, during their marriage and while raising their children, often taught school to help maintain a secure home life for us. Mom's opinions and beliefs were the guidelines with which we lived. When her interest in spirituality arose, she pursued the art of learning to live a spiritual life with the right vibrations and a clear mind. She approached this with the same vigor and determination she had displayed as a young woman pursuing a career. She was confident that all our problems could be solved through various mystic means, one of those being recognizing problems that could originate from a past life that cluttered our minds in the present.

I always enjoyed our adult to adult conversations. While I had always humored her, and had a passing interest in her concepts, I never thought of applying any of them to my day to day existence.

I remembered the birth of my son, Michael, and how she had

told me who he had been in his previous life. She told me what his name had been and that he had lived in northern California. Mom had been working with a group of people who were learning to clear the mind. She said Michael had belonged to a branch of this same group. And where did she get this information? "From Michael," she said. She explained that she could "talk" telepathically to my two-month old son. I tried unsuccessfully to picture Michael's thought waves as I looked at my husky blond-haired son, gurgling to himself, as he lay in his crib.

Months later, she had talked to a lady who edited a small newsletter for this group. She told Mom she remembered writing up a death announcement for this man who was now my son. This story fascinated me, but I never had reason to question her in depth about past lives. However, I was now desperate.

The children's welcome ran itself out, and my mother and I were finally left alone over cake and coffee. She lost no time in asking me what problem I had that couldn't be discussed over the phone.

Hesitantly, I edged into my story by telling her how I was still feeling sad three years after John Lennon's death; that I was constantly listening to his music, although I had not done so before 1980; that all of this was driving me crazy. Maybe there was something to this psychic business which could explain why I had been feeling and acting this way? With a feeling of total helplessness, I stopped my rambling.

Mother took a deep breath and closed her eyes, not moving a muscle, for several minutes.

She began to speak slowly and with deliberation. "I do see something . . . I see you, as a young girl . . . in England . . . the 1400s . . . betrothed to a man who in this life was John Lennon. He is sick and is taken away . . . he does not return . . . he dies . . . I see a cart coming for him . . . you are most distressed and you die shortly afterward."

Questions buzzed through my mind. "What were our names?"

Mother, eyes still closed, said, "Your last name was St. James . . ."

"And my name was Katherine, and he was John . . . right?" I couldn't believe the names Katherine and John came to me like they did, but as soon as I had uttered them, I knew these names were correct.

"Yes . . . Katherine St. James and John . . . John Baron. And you lived near a place . . . sounds like . . . Castlemere."

"And Katherine's father and mother?"

"Her father's name was Robert . . . Robert St. James."

"Where is this place, Castlemere?"

"England . . . near Salisbury Plain . . . I see white cliffs, fog, and lush green grass."

Lush green grass! That was what I had seen surrounding the milestone when I had first listened to *Jealous Guy*.

"Quick, come with me," and to my mother's surprise I went to the stereo, letting the sounds of *Jealous Guy* fill the room. "Tell me if you can pick up anything from this song, okay?"

When the melody ended, my mother only said, "This song is written about this life in ancient England. He seems to be talking about his death. Oh, and I could hear chimes, not in the song, but I could hear them in my mind; there were chimes where you lived."

It was as if my three-year-old cloud had disintegrated and drifted away in a million wisps; everything seemed clearer. I had actually known him! I found myself laughing and crying, asking my mother why I had taken so long to tell her of my grief.

"Everything happens in its own good time. Three years ago you weren't ready for answers because you didn't know the questions. Besides, people only question Life when they are ready to hear more."

Therefore, in the spring of 1984, I was now ready to hear answers, to accept that I was once Katherine St. James who had loved a John Baron—but only on one condition—that I could prove it.

Five

On a Sunday afternoon in April, after a late breakfast, I summoned the courage to share with Bob my mother's explanation of my prolonged, inexplicable grief.

Bob stared at me as if I had lost my mind. "Are you saying you are connected to the *Imagine* album?" he snorted.

"No," I tried to explain, "not the album . . . a song from the album . . . *Jealous Guy.*"

"I don't understand what you are getting at. What, exactly, are you talking about?"

"Mom saw that I had known John Lennon in another life and . . ."

"Well, that explains it, doesn't it? For Christ's sake, Jewelle, she's always got some kooky idea. You can just add this one to the list."

"Look, I was the one who asked her if I had known him in another life. It didn't come easy, asking her. It's nothing I can touch or see, but I feel so . . . oh, forget it!" I was mumbling and humiliated. How could I tell my husband that I loved another man from another century?

By the next day, I had mostly recuperated from Bob's stinging words. I knew that he scoffed at spiritual ideas, and that accepting new ideas, with no proof, was impossible for him. And when my mother was the one giving me the information, it was doubly hard to convince him of any validity in the whole thing.

Bob's own upbringing had been with a Naval Petty Officer father who was often away, and a mother who raised her children virtually alone, yet in the unseen shadow of her husband's conservative values.

I knew my own upbringing had its flaws stemming from my mother's determination that we become as spiritual as humanly possible. My first recollection was eating only health food in a time when doing so was being "a health food nut." Luckily, I found a friend at school who ate dried kelp at recess and never drank milk!

In my teens, Mother connected with a different group of friends who performed therapy on each other to rid themselves of past upsets and physical and mental pains. Their theory was that to clear the mind allowed a person's true and good personality to emerge. After many of Mother's sessions it was apparent that she had developed psychic abilities. She stressed that these abilities had been hidden, but because she had gotten rid of her mental "garbage" they were now able to surface more clearly. She also insisted that if everyone cleared their minds they, too, would be naturally psychic.

Over the years a good portion of our family, including my father, my aunts, cousins, and even my grandmother, would speak of extraordinary happenings as everyday occurrences.

As a young adult I soon learned that most of the world doesn't openly discuss the reasons why people react the way they do or consider that maybe most people's problems stem from their soul's past. And when, at age sixteen, I went to live with an aunt who was not spiritually minded, I saw how others lived with down-to-earth ideals and were still happy with their lives.

So, when Bob openly scoffed at my mother's "kooky ideas," I was once again torn between what I had learned and what I thought a logical person with a normal upbringing would think.

I was so unsure of myself. Maybe Bob had a point. I may have agreed with him except I couldn't discount the loneliness and loss I felt for this man, John Baron/Lennon. I had to prove to myself without a doubt whether I had known and loved the soul most recently know as John Lennon. I wouldn't try to explain anymore to Bob or anyone else until I was able to explain it to myself. After all, it was I who needed to know the truth.

With Bob and the children safely at work and school, I ignored the lure of the early morning sunshine and retreated to a corner of our basement. I blew the dust off an atlas of the world and carefully turned the pages until I found England. After an hour of tracing my finger over the names of hundreds of cities and villages, searching for Castlemere, blurring vision and an aching back forced me to give up.

With a fresh cup of coffee in hand, I went out into the sunshine. I mentally reviewed the visualized scene my mother had sketched for me just days earlier.

In the medieval English village Castlemere, a young Katherine St. James, daughter of Robert St. James, merchant, had fallen in love with and was to marry John Baron, son of the local gentry. The young couple had spent hours walking in green countryside or sitting in the small garden adjacent to the St. James' home. Wherever they were, the sound of chimes was always present. Somewhere in the area were white cliffs surrounded by thick, gray fog. Shortly before the nuptial date, John fell ill. Arrangements were made for his transport to a rest home. On their last afternoon spent together, Katherine and John sat in the garden, oblivious to the cool October wind, awaiting the cart which was to take him away from her. As the horse drew the cart to a stop, John took Katherine's hand and whispered, "Please remember . . . always remember our love."

There were so few clues. I had no luck finding Castlemere on the map of England. How could I find any trace of the Baron and St. James families if I could not first locate where they had lived?

Impulsively I grabbed my purse and car keys, and drove to the public library. There I checked out an armful of books bearing titles like, *Medieval England, History of the British Isles, Life in the Fifteenth Century,* and *Lost Villages of Britain.*

I spent the long, hot days of that summer as a devoted student of English history. For hours on end, I devoured accounts of past life in England. I entered the worlds of lords and ladies, knights in shining armor, and whole class systems living and dying in draughty, cold castles. I sympathized with the lot of the lower classes on whose toil, hunger, and suffering the prosperity of the privileged was built. I learned the stories of Henry VIII, Anne Boleyn, Bloody Mary, Elizabeth I, Oliver Cromwell, the Plague—all those fascinating stories which somehow slipped by me in school. I loved learning this colorful history, but nowhere was there mention of a town called Castlemere or families bearing the names of Baron or St. James.

Then one hot afternoon, late in August, I stuffed the children into the car, surrounded them with stacks of books, and headed out for one more trek. While the children were having their daily swim, I struggled into the library with my huge stack of books. The librarian, a kindly older woman, was looking at me, curiosity written all over her face. For some time she had wondered why I was checking out so many history books.

"What are you studying?" she asked.

"I'm not studying really . . . I'm just trying to find information about some people who lived in Medieval times."

"What people?"

"Uh . . . ancestors."

Her face lit up. "Oh, you're doing genealogy!" When she saw my puzzled expression, she added, "Family trees."

I jumped at that, still not quite sure what she meant. I was ushered to a shelf of books I had not investigated. At once I saw that it was histories of families, rather than histories of countries, that I wanted. The librarian asked what period I was researching. When I told her the 1400s, her eyebrows registered surprise and she explained that most amateur researchers have difficulty discovering ancestors earlier than the 1700s. How could I explain that I had not gone past any century, but had just landed shakily in the 1400s?

"If none of these are of any help, I suggest you phone the *Jesus Christ of Latter Day Saints Historical Society*. They have copies of parish records from all over the world and they offer help to anyone who is researching their own families. Genealogists would be lost without them."

Rummaging through her stack of references, she found the telephone number of the Kelowna branch and gave it to me. As an afterthought she added, "We have microfiche lent to us by the *L.D.S. Church* that you would be welcome to look at." She gestured to a room at the back of the library.

"Any time you would like to look at them, I'll show you how to operate the microfiche readers."

On the drive home I was fascinated by the idea of looking at ancient records right here in our local library. But would I find my ancient people? Had they ever existed?

As soon as I got home, I dialed the *L.D.S.* number and attempted to explain my quest to the woman who took my call.

When I spoke of Castlemere, England, in the 1400s, she expressed surprise, and said that the books she needed were at her home. After having me repeat the particulars, she requested I phone again in a couple of days and ask for Glynis.

"Oh, and in the meantime, send me your family group sheets. It will help me know where to begin."

I broke into a sweat. What in *hell* were family group sheets?

35

Six

I sat for some time at my kitchen table agonizing over how I would go about producing family group sheets when I was clueless about what they were. Realizing I had no choice, and dreading another dead end, I telephoned Glynis and blurted, "This is Jewelle . . . I'm sorry but I wasn't totally honest with you earlier. You see, I am not researching my family tree. I've been told by a psychic that I had lived a past life near Castlemere, as a girl named Katherine St. James, whose father was Robert St. James, and with a man named John Baron—all who lived in England around 1430 . . ."

This was met by laughter from the other end of the line. Then Glynis confided that after talking to me, she had wondered how I managed to trace my family back to the fifteenth century without previously using their reference facilities.

Glynis explained that family group sheets were a recording of your family tree, starting with yourself and working your way backwards. An expert genealogist would end up with hundreds of "grandparents" over many generations.

I plunged on, asking her if she would help me. There was a pause before she said, "As a Mormon I'm not supposed to believe in reincarnation but, because of my husband, I do." She told me that her husband could describe in detail Moscow's

Red Square but, because he had never been there, the only logical explanation they had was that he lived there in a previous life. Glynis promised to help me all she could, and requested a few days to research Castlemere.

My watch told me I had no time to savor this piece of good luck. It was time to fetch the kids from the pool. I was about to leave when the telephone rang. Had Glynis found Castlemere already?

"Hi, what's new?" It was Debbie suggesting with the kids returning to school on Tuesday, we could spend the day shopping and go for lunch. It only took me seconds to agree and set the time.

The back-to-school ritual occupied the next few days as I was caught up in the annual frenzy of readying wardrobes and buying school supplies.

One afternoon, as I sat in the beauty salon waiting for my girls to have their hair cut, I noticed a poster announcing that a psychic, Cecilia, was coming that evening and sessions could be arranged by appointment. As I paid the stylist for the hair cuts, I hesitantly asked where the psychic would be. "Right here in the salon," she replied. I impulsively made an appointment.

After dinner, nervous and excited, I informed Bob that I was going out for about an hour and that I was seeing a psychic. I hoped he would not question my reasons. He did not.

Driving through the dark streets to the salon, my mind buzzed with questions to ask. By the time I arrived at the door, however, I found I had none. What would I say? I could just imagine the reaction to the opening line, "Hi, I'm Jewelle, John Lennon's medieval lover. Tell me more!"

The friendly woman who greeted me motioned me to follow her into a room behind the salon. She invited me to sit at a small oval table. While she lit a plain white candle, she introduced herself as Cecilia and confirmed that I was Jewelle.

"I've never been to a psychic before," I heard myself saying, "except, of course, my mother who is psychic . . . but she's my mother so that doesn't really count does it?" I stopped, realizing that I was babbling.

Cecilia smiled as she took my hand, examining the lines in my palm. *"Ah, I see a few stormy years when you were in your teens . . . finding your niche in life. You have developed into a stable, well-rounded lady. Your life with your husband and children is happy and secure. Yet . . . I see an underlying problem within your heart . . . you belong with a man from long ago . . . he is someone you have not connected with for many lifetimes. It is as if you are always in the wrong place at the wrong time. Now . . . just a minute . . . I am getting someone here with you . . . a male. Did you have a friend who died in an auto accident?"*

"Yes."

"He says to tell you that he is with you and is trying to help you. Do you understand that message?"

"No."

"He says you will in time."

". . . back to this man I'm "connected to " . . . will I meet him in my next life?"

"You will meet him in this life through some sort of meditation."

I thought sardonically, 'This lifetime . . . John Lennon . . . oh sure!'

"Do you have any other questions before we finish?"

"Yes, just one . . . this man . . . the one I haven't been connecting with . . . can you see what he was doing in his last life?"

Cecilia paused briefly before saying, *"I can only see one aspect of his last life . . . music."*

Bob greeted me with, "Well, what did the crystal ball reveal?" in a tone that was at once both sarcastic and curious.

"Oh, it said I'm married to a tall, dark, sexy man who has more brains than money."

"In that case, I'm glad it wasn't a waste of time," he smiled.

I slept soundly that night, quickly entering the hazy world of dreams. My surroundings became crystal clear. I was walking over soft green rolling hills . . . someone was holding my hand . . . it was Patrick!

"I shouldn't be here," he said, "but I wanted to spend a minute with you."

"Patrick, I've missed you . . . oh, it's good to see you . . . to hear your voice . . . are you alright?"

He stared at me, his warm eyes intense. "Jewelle, put foxglove on my grave."

Some men were approaching and instinctively I knew that Patrick was in danger. He was not supposed to be here.

I screamed for him to run. Instantly he was gone, and the beautiful field with him.

Gasping for air, I sat upright.

A cold trickle of sweat worked its way down my spine. From beside me I heard Bob groggily asking me what was wrong. I told him I had had a dream, and asked him what foxglove was.

"Huh?"

"What's foxglove?"

"A flower."

"Does it grow here?"

"Some I guess, but mostly on Vancouver Island . . . brought there by the British . . . Jesus, Jewelle! It's four o'clock in the morning."

I lay, staring at the ceiling, wondering if I had had a dream or had Patrick actually been there? And why had Patrick told me to put foxglove on his grave? How could I have dreamed of a flower I had never heard of? And how could I have remembered exactly how his voice had sounded after all these years?

Seven

When Debbie's Camaro turned into the driveway the next morning, I waved goodbye to the children and wished them a good day at school. I hopped into Debbie's car, and was glad to see her in a good mood. In unison, we laughingly declared our gratitude for the beginning of school and having survived another summer break. As we cruised along the highway in a companionable silence, I felt a compulsive urge to share details of the experiences I had bottled up for so long.

"I went to a psychic the other day," I started, "and I think I knew John Lennon in another life in England." Before I knew it, I had told Debbie how I had suffered over Lennon's death and how I was trying to find some answers to my nagging questions.

Debbie's face was blank. She registered nothing in response to what I had just spilled out. She was going to tell me I was nuts! Then, with a trace of understanding in her voice, Debbie asked, "Is that why you wrote that letter to the newspaper?"

I shrugged, and told her about the strange dream I had about Patrick White, saying it was really weird because after all these years I had forgotten what his voice sounded like.

"What did he say?"

"He told me to put foxglove on his grave."

"That's creepy," Debbie said.

"I know," I said wistfully. "You'd think after all these years, if he was going to contact me, he would mention the baby. I mean, that's our connection, not some flower called fox-glove . . ." I trailed off.

Our conversation turned lighter, and for the first time in months I felt carefree and frivolous as we browsed our way through the shops. Hours later, burdened with packages and suffering from sore feet, we lucked upon a bistro.

"Caesar salad!"

"Cheesecake!"

Seated at an oval table, surrounded by lush green plants and soft music, we sipped wine and dallied over our sinful lunch. Without warning, tears sprang to my eyes and the relaxed mood was broken. "I've never said this to anyone, but I miss John so much sometimes I think I'll die."

Although I thought she was probably thinking, "for Christ's sake," Debbie kept a straight face and said, "It sounds like a puzzle and you have to find all the missing pieces."

I had not thought of it as a puzzle and confessed that I had a lot of pieces to find.

"You'll find them," whispered Debbie.

I wondered to myself, is she thinking that my life has become so boring that I am inventing lives with rock stars and teenage heart throbs?

As we were about to get in the car, I noticed a small shop on the opposite side of the street. The sign on the window simply read, *Posters*. For some reason I had to go in. Leaving Debbie standing beside her opened car door, I dodged traffic and dashed into the store. I hastily scanned the racks of posters until I found one of the Beatles. Even though it was of disappointing quality, I took it to the counter. There, an elderly man sitting on a stool looked at my choice. He studied me intently and shuffled to the rear of the store. "Hang on a minute, lady. I have something for you back here."

He emerged, unrolling another Beatles poster. This was a beautiful one which commemorated their *Royal Command Performance* in 1963. "This is for you. I just got it from New York."

Feeling somewhat bewildered, I asked the price expecting an exorbitant figure. I scarcely believed the five dollar quote and had to ask him to repeat it.

Moments later I was in the car, both posters securely beside me. I was relieved when Debbie turned on the radio, eliminating the need to talk. All the way home I wondered why that storekeeper had kept such a good poster in the back when posters were all he sold, and why had he sold it to me for such a low price when the rest were twice the cost?

That night, as I tucked the children into bed, I asked each about their first day at school.

Twelve-year-old Joanne did not want to talk about school. Her face bore a puzzled expression. "Mom, someone is hanging around me . . . just watching me."

"At school? Dammit, this happens every September at schools . . . did you tell your teacher? I'm going to phone the principal."

"Mom, not at school, here . . . at home . . . it's not a person . . . it's a spirit . . . a man spirit . . ."

Instantly relieved, I had a second to breathe freely before I realized exactly what she had said. "A spirit?" I had to swallow hard and ask calmly what this "spirit" looked like.

Joanne, in a matter of fact way, stated that he was wearing "spectacles." "He's real small. Well, maybe he just looks small because he's at a distance. Up there." She pointed above our heads.

"Can you see anything else besides spectacles?" I thought spectacles was an old fashioned word for Joanne to use for glasses.

Joanne replied, "He has a funny hat. It's plaid with a pom-pom on it. Beige shorts with elastic bottoms, plaid knee-high socks, and black shoes with buckles."

"Strange outfit," we both laughed.

Joanne suddenly said, "I know that hat. It's like a Sherlock Holmes hat!"

The spirit suddenly seemed a friendly sort, though I wasn't really convinced there *was* a spirit. However, it was light entertainment for a mother whose daughter was beginning that estranged pre-teen age.

"Who is this spirit? Does he have a name?" I asked, humoring her.

"I don't know."

"Well, ask!"

Joanne closed her eyes briefly before she replied, "Mom, it's John Lennon!"

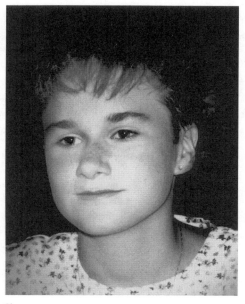

Joanne, age 12

Eight

"John Lennon? Are you sure?" I asked, no longer humoring her.

I didn't want to startle her but, as I looked at her calm little face, I realized I was the startled one.

"How can you see him?"

"Because he wants me to see him."

"Is he here right now?"

"Yes."

My mind raced. While wanting to grab the moment, I didn't want to frighten or confuse her. As calmly as I could, I explained that I was going to ask her a few questions to ask the spirit. It was unlikely she would know the answers. Perhaps the John spirit could supply the answers for her.

"Can you tell me the name of John Lennon's mother?"

" . . . Lia or something sounding like that."

"It was Julia," I supplied. "John had an aunt who raised him. Can you name her?"

All Joanne could supply was the letter "M." "It's like M . . . M . . . M . . ." (Lennon's aunt's name is Mimi.)

For John's uncle's name she correctly responded, "George!"

"When is John Lennon's birthday?" She indicated July, then October. (John Lennon was born October 9, 1940.)

44

Although I was amazed that my little girl was giving me the information so effortlessly, I recalled having read about this kind of interview. Some perceptive people can, evidently, pick up the thoughts of the person questioning them and parrot them back. I decided to test this out by asking Joanne questions about my own childhood. "When I was your age, Joanne, and in elementary school, I had a best friend. What was her name?"

Joanne responded with Pamela. The correct answer was Terri. I followed with a similar question about my friend Daphne, whom I saw only in the summer holidays. Joanne gave me Lisa. After I had asked a few more related questions, I was sure she was not picking up anything from me. All questions she had answered about John Lennon had been totally or partially correct yet all her responses concerning me were incorrect.

"Is John still here right now?" I asked.

At Joanne's nod I asked her if she could tell me anything that would convince me he was actually present.

"Just . . . he hopes you like the poster, Mom."

I was still gulping from that comment when Joanne yawned, announced she was bored, and wanted to go to sleep.

Over the next few days I sat with Joanne and asked her questions about John. I slowly became convinced that her information really was coming from John Lennon. Her answers were too specific, and her vocabulary was not that of my twelve-year-old daughter.

In this same period my mother had been trying to convince me to join her friend's organization. She was sure that the best way for me to discover my past lives was to clear my mind of all its upsets.

But although I accepted her psychic abilities, I wasn't ready to join a group that had a bearing on my childhood quest to remain "normal." However, I had always believed that Mother knew best. Torn between her knowledge and my desire to learn about John and Katherine's past, yet wishing to retain my independence, I posed my questions to Joanne.

"Joanne, would you ask John if I should join up with Grandma's friends . . . if it will help me to find out more about our English life?"

Joanne simply stated, "John says it doesn't matter whether or not you join Grandma's friends. It doesn't matter what you do, you and he will always be together. And it doesn't matter how you search your past life. All you have to do is ask to receive the answers."

For a brief second, in response to Joanne's statement, I had an inner knowing that this conversation was a gift from the spirit world.

Another day I asked her how John was able to reach so many people through his ability to write wonderful music.

"John says it was his given job. Everybody has a job to do . . . but everyone is also given help if they require it. He says he had an ability to write music and perform . . . but some music was *given* to him." Joanne looked confused. "Mom, how could someone else give him music . . . why would they do that?"

I didn't want to tell her that I suspected the "someone" was a spirit, so I nonchalantly said, "Let's just ask him who gave him this music, okay?"

The little girl grimaced. "John had a teacher who had always helped him with his music. Through this teacher he has grown to love waltzes."

"Does this teacher have a name?"

"Johann."

My mind raced. Waltzes . . . Johann . . . "Is this Johann Strauss?" I asked Joanne.

Joanne paused for a minute, then said, "Yes, Johann says that's how people knew him." The girl looked puzzled. "Mom, who is this Strauss guy?"

"A man who wrote beautiful music . . ." I trailed off not knowing what to think, yet feeling a sense of overwhelming awe.

By now I was getting used to Joanne's unexpected answers. I suppose it should have been mind boggling, but instead I had an overwhelming sense of pride for John and what he had accomplished. I also felt he had more than completed any job that the Universe may have assigned him.

"One more thing, Mom. Your job is part of this too. Your job is to continue John's work by keeping people aware of him. If they remember him, they will also remember the messages he tried to give the world through his music."

I smiled. 'Oh yeah, right,' I thought, 'I'll just be telling everyone that I'm a messenger of John's. Maybe I should also announce that I've seen Elvis at the local supermarket!'

I started to wonder seriously about what I was supposed to do with this information. Was it meant to be kept quiet? It made me think of the messages in John's music. What use would they have been if he had kept them to himself? Did his music even belong to him? Did my knowledge of these conversations with Joanne or this emerging story belong to me or was I supposed to share it? Little did I know it then, but these questions stayed with me for many years.

One day, a few weeks after Joanne had first seen John Lennon, she announced that she didn't want to talk with John anymore. (Joanne explained to me, nearly two decades later, although the memory of her experience was hazy, she does recall feeling frustrated, possibly by a change of energy enveloping her as she communicated with John.) I had to respect her decision, and considered myself lucky for those few precious weeks that I was able to communicate with John through her.

Then, one day, I heard from Glynis when the postman delivered a large, brown envelope. In it were copies of ancient maps

47

of all the English counties. In addition there was a short history about the origins of the Baron family and a description of the lives of medieval peasants and noblemen. Glynis had included a postscript saying she was unable to find Castlemere or a St. James family from that era. She concluded by promising to keep in touch with me.

Another autumn arrived and with it a Thanksgiving Day, whose deep blue skies perfectly framed the vividly golden foliage of the forest and the mountain's azure slopes. Sated by their turkey dinner, the children abandoned Bob and me. We lingered over glasses of wine. I had waited some weeks for the opportunity to catch Bob in a mellow mood. "Bob, I want to go to England."

"Yeah, right!" was his laughing response. When I insisted that I was serious, he held up the bottle and asked me how much wine I'd had. Determined not to get annoyed, I plunged ahead saying I did not mean right away, but that I had to go find where Katherine and John had lived.

Exasperated, he countered, "Where in England? You can't just go over there with no destination. Besides, it will take years to save that kind of money." To that I stubbornly replied that I would save for years if I had to, and begged him to try and understand. The topic was dropped when Bob suggested we discuss it again when I got the money.

Over the next few days I unsuccessfully tried to think of ways I could earn the money for a trip to England without becoming a working mother. Intending to pick her brain, I invited Debbie to come over for coffee.

"England? Why would you want to go to England?" I was taken aback by her reaction. Surely Debbie had understood when I poured out the whole story to her on our shopping trip? I quoted her earlier remark of the puzzle I had to put together. "Did I say that?" she asked.

Then the door opened and Bob strode over to the table. He laid a large, flat parcel in front of me. He kissed me and said, "Surprise!" When I ripped open the paper, I found he had taken my Beatles poster and had it mounted and framed. It looked just wonderful!

That evening, I telephoned my mother to tell her of my idea to travel to England. She suggested I invite my sister to go along. She meant Korinn, of course. Konni could not manage such a trip.

I have two sisters. Korinn is the younger one. She is quiet, easy going, and always ready for adventure. Her sunny disposition matches her fair hair and twinkling deep blue eyes. My other sister, Konni, moved to California after she married an American. Multiple Sclerosis had confined her to home, and it hurt me to visualize Konni's thin body in a wheelchair. I wondered if she could still manage her long dark hair. Expensive airfare limited family visits while tapes replaced phone calls.

Mom was right. I wouldn't want to travel alone to another country. Korinn would be perfect. My baby sister was young, single, and intrigued with my English past. But why was I thinking about traveling anywhere when I hadn't saved a dime?

My mother, pointing out that my call was costing money, was about to say goodbye, but I had something to ask.

"Could you look at something psychically for me? I probably shouldn't have done it," I said, "but I confided my feelings about John Lennon to Debbie back in the fall. She seemed to understand, but today she acted weird. She acted the same way when I wrote a letter to the paper just after he died. She seems hostile towards him and I don't know why."

My mother said that she "got the picture," and she'd be out for a visit soon. We would talk then.

I had barely hung up the phone when it rang.

Glynis said excitedly, "Jewelle, I've found your Castlemere!"

Nine

Castlemere existed!

Long pent-up questions tumbled out of me. Glynis responded by saying she had been doing research about Stonehenge in the south of England when she came across a passage in a book written by Celia Fiennes, who traveled throughout England between 1685 to 1718. The passage read, *"From Stonehenge I went to Evell (Yeovil) in Somersetshire thence to Meer (Mere), a little town; by the town is a vast hill called the Castle of Meer, its now all grass over and so steepe that the ascent is by footsteps cut in the side of the hill . . ."*

Was this my Castlemere? Well, it was all I had to go on. Castlemere was actually the Castle of Mere, located in the town of Mere. Glynis added that Mere borders the Salisbury Plain near Stonehenge in the county of Wiltshire.

I now had a focal point—a destination. All I had to do was find proof that a Katherine St. James or a John Baron had lived there.

Over the next several weeks I tried to research Wiltshire in the fifteenth century, but other than information on the ancient rings of stone, Stonehenge, there wasn't much.

Then one day, as I was leaving the library, I picked up a pamphlet entitled, *Tracing Your Roots*. Observing me with the pamphlet, the librarian assured me that it was an interesting course in genealogy. It occurred to me that such a course might teach me a method for verifying the existence of Katherine St. James and John Baron and their association with Mere.

That evening my mother phoned to tell me she was delaying her visit. Christmas was not that far away; she would come and visit then. With some hesitation, she added that she had taken a psychic look at Debbie's seemingly hostile attitude toward John Lennon and her lack of compassion toward my obvious pain. "I don't like to cause trouble between the two of you. You have been friends for so long . . . and maybe it won't even be of any help."

Not about to let her get away with that, I demanded details.

"Well, the whole picture wasn't very clear, but I saw Debbie as having been in the same ancient life as you . . . she seems to have been a house servant for the St. James family. One thing I saw was John waiting for you—for Katherine—in the garden. Debbie, or whoever she was, approached him, making eyes at him. When he just sneered at her and walked away, she was most insulted.

"I would say you're dealing with someone who has her own memories of a past life. These memories aren't like the memories you and Debbie share of your old high school days together. Past life memories, if a person isn't aware of them, emerge as feelings rather than mental recollections. And sometimes these feelings can be disturbing. Jewelle, remember that unexplainable grief you felt when John Lennon was shot? Well, that was a past life feeling. You had no past memory of having loved and lost, but you did have the feelings. This is no different with Debbie. For reasons beyond her logical control, she feels very uncomfortable when you mention John Lennon. Remember, that our present relationships with others, our feelings, our loves, and our hates often survive the passage of time."

Finally, it was Christmas morning, 1984. Bob and I snuggled under the covers, listening to the children's squeals of delight as their stockings were emptied. I was fumbling around for my slippers when Bob stopped me. Still lying in bed, he produced a narrow box wrapped in silver paper. "I want to give you this before we face the mob."

As I opened the present, I sensed that Bob was somehow giving this gift to himself as well as me. In the box was a British Airways ticket—Vancouver to London. Through my tears, I listed the obstacles: where did he get the money? who would look after the kids? With a laugh and a hug he said, "It's all taken care of. I'll book my holidays for September and play mom for a while. Please note that it's a return ticket and you will be coming back." I realized that he hoped that if I made the trip, I would get the whole John Lennon thing out of my system.

I had no idea whether discovering the existence of John and Katherine would bring me peace. I could only visualize traveling to England, having all my questions answered. I made plans with Korinn, who lived in Vancouver, to accompany me. With months to anticipate our trip, I planned the itinerary so that we would spend the first week in London playing tourist, then traveling to Salisbury, the largest centre near Mere.

I immersed myself in the genealogy course as one way of passing the time, and quickly found the classes hypnotic. The instructor guided us back in time, and soon I regarded myself as having been transformed from an amateur, looking for instant answers, to an avid and thorough researcher.

I learned about my own family's roots. My father's side, Norwegian; my mother's father, Swedish; my mother's mother who emphatically stressed, "Don't ask me my ancestry. I am Canadian." My grandma reminded us that she was born in Victoria at the turn of the century and her parents, who were married in

B.C., were also born in Canada. "How dare people not accept Canadian as my nationality?" she would ask.

As the time for our departure drew near I found myself thinking of our sister, Konni. When was the last time I had even talked to her? To help dispel the feelings of guilt I had about living a normal life while she was held prisoner by her illness, I got out my tape recorder and began to talk. After a slow start with family news, I told her about Korinn and me flying to England. Soon I was telling her my reasons for going, and how Mom had seen my past life with John Lennon. Having nothing more to say, I filled the remainder of the tape with *Jealous Guy*. I packaged up the tape and dropped it in the nearest mailbox.

Our momentous departure day in September, 1985, arrived, and Korinn and I took our first international flight from Vancouver to London.

Once we were airborne, Korinn remarked that my mood seemed to match the wet, gloomy Vancouver weather. Wasn't I glad to finally be on our way? But I couldn't shake my apprehension. What if Mere isn't the right place? What if there are no Barons or St. James there? For Korinn's sake, I shook myself out of my funk, and tried to enjoy the British Airways flight.

Many hours later, we dragged ourselves through the interminable customs process. For the tenth time since we started our descent to Heathrow Airport, Korinn giggled. "I just can't believe that we are in England."

I echoed her excitement, but for different reasons. Despite my restlessness to search for my past, and with Mere only days away, I put matters into perspective and concentrated on the first leg of our trip—being a tourist in London.

The next day, reassured by the claim we could not get lost on the Tube, we ventured forth and were soon in awe of this fabulous city. We were thrilled by the changing of the Buckingham Palace Guards, shuddered in the infamous Tower of London, and reveled at the night lights of Piccadilly Circus. I wrote postcards home, knowing Bob would have loved London.

At last it was time to leave London and catch the morning train to Salisbury. Blue skies and warm air greeted us as we arrived and registered at the Victorian White Horse Hotel, with its charming white lace curtains and window boxes overflowing with vibrantly colored flowers.

Our bags were scarcely deposited in our room when I was on my way to the Tourist Information Centre. I lost no time asking the young woman there questions about Mere.

"Mere? Why would you want to go there? There's so much to see right here in Salisbury! We have our Cathedral, which has the tallest spire in England. We have Old Sarum, the original part of Salisbury . . ."

Patiently, I broke through her tourist promotion and indicated that I wanted to go to Mere for family research, and asked her for a bus schedule. In response, she told me there was but one bus a week to Mere, leaving on Tuesdays and returning to Salisbury on Fridays. "But I'll be flying home before Tuesday," I said incredulously.

The young woman shrugged dismissively. Then she recalled a woman who conducted tours for the Centre and would be at the White Hart Hotel at 4:00 p.m. to arrange the next day's tour. Perhaps we could make arrangements with her.

I contained my frustration with the travel problem until I found Korinn outside basking in the sunshine. Her response was to point out the half-timbered public house, advertising fresh scones topped with strawberries and thick Devon cream.

"What if I can't get to Mere? Maybe I'll have to get a cab. I wonder how much that would cost? It's over twenty miles from here!"

Over strawberries and cream, Korinn sensibly suggested we go and see the tour lady first. She kept me on an even keel until we headed to the White Hart Hotel.

In the miniature garden behind the Tudor hotel, we joined a lively group of people clustered around a woman who was explaining how she conducted tours by trying to include everyone's request with the area of the map she displayed. I added my request to visit Mere.

"Mere . . . no one has asked me to go there before, but we should be able to fit it in."

The next morning, replete with a genuine English breakfast, we boarded a rugged looking van and headed out across the green Salisbury Plain toward Stonehenge. Four other women accompanied us on our journey.

When we arrived at the Druid monument, the air was still and mysterious. I stood in awe of the ancient gray stones that loomed before us. For several seconds it seemed as if time had frozen. A warm flow of energy embraced me and then, just as abruptly, the feeling was gone, leaving me with the mystical rings of stone. The presence had been so close . . . so personal. *(Years later, I learned that my mystical feelings at Stonehenge had also been experienced by numerous visitors at the ancient stone ring.)*

Our guide announced that our next stop would be Stourhead Gardens. As Mere was close by, she would drop the others off at the Gardens and then drive Korinn and me to Mere. Between her commentaries about the country through which we traveled, I was fascinated by her statement that her own family roots were traceable to earliest English history.

Beyond Stourhead, the road narrowed and wound its way between miles of hedgerows bordering green fields. We rounded a corner, and without warning we were in the village of Mere.

Stopping the van in a tiny square, our guide pointed out the tourist information office. "The chap who works there will be helpful. I suggest you talk to him. I'll be back to pick you up in about an hour."

She was about to leave when she saw me staring at an enormous grass covered mountain that stood off in the distance. To my unasked question she said, "That is what was once the Castle of Mere. A fortress built, I think, in the 1200s, maybe earlier."

With that, she drove off leaving me numb with the realization that I had come all this way, only to have a single hour. All I was able to do was look briefly at the mountain, Castlemere. There was no time to do more than that.

I was about to succumb to hysterics because of the short amount of time when Korinn said, "We have a whole hour, let's make the most of it."

At the tiny tourist office we found a big, burly, red-headed man who greeted us pleasantly. When I explained I was doing family research, he offered to help. To my first question concerning St. James families in Mere, his response was negative. To Baron, he offered that a Baron family has lived in Mere for the last few hundred years. "I suggest you see the Vicar. He can tell you more. Here, I'll show you where he lives."

He strode out of the little office with us in his wake. He pointed up a tiny cobblestone lane, toward a residence near the parish church.

As I tried to absorb my surroundings, I contained my excitement of the news that Barons had lived here. Korinn must have read my mind, for as we left the tiny square she began shooting off a roll of film.

The whole village seemed to be a sea of stone; stone of different types and shades. Surrounding the square was a radius of small shops, a library, and a museum. I soon learned that I had chosen mid-week closing day, and I realized how totally unprepared I was. I hadn't researched properly and here I was paying the price. So, not only did I mess up finding out about proper transportation, I had also picked a day when not even the museum was open. I had just assumed everything would fall into place with a few precise questions. Now I had to face facts—I had less than one hour to find a family who may have lived here five hundred years ago. I could have cried, but there was no time for that!

Bees humming seemed to be the only sign of life as we walked quickly past stone cottages. The heavy scent of roses assailed us as I rapped on the heavy oak door of the vicarage.

A pleasant, middle-aged woman greeted us with the information that the Vicar was out. Would we like to come in and wait for his return? Barely able to hide my impatience, I explained that our time was limited, I was doing a family history, and I needed to visit the cemetery. She pointed the way along a short lane bordered by a stone wall creeping with roses.

We couldn't find the gate, and time was ticking away. Laughing and shrieking we climbed over the rock wall, tumbling to the other side. A light wind blew across the field of headstones as I began searching for a stone bearing the Baron name. There seemed to be no monument dated prior to 1800. Just as I was about to ask for help from an elderly caretaker, I saw a tall thin man approaching us from across the cemetery. Pushing his long dark hair from his eyes, the middle-aged man breathlessly introduced himself as the Vicar and expressed his eagerness to be of assistance. Conscious of the rapidly evaporating time I stole a look at my watch, and quickly repeated the object of my visit.

"Yes, I am familiar with the Baron name. Come to the church and I will show you something interesting." The Vicar pointed to a stone church standing in the distance. Despite the beautiful blue sky and the hedges of roses swaying gently in the warm breezy air, the church seemed to loom moodily in the distance like a creation from a Brontë novel. Korinn and I smiled at each other as we left for St. Michael's Church with the Vicar, this time through the gate!

We could scarcely breathe the cold, damp air as we entered the stone building. Pointing to the black flagstones on the floor of the church, the Vicar pointed out one inscribed: *John Baron*, son of Randolph Baron, died in 1718.

I felt weak as I stared at the name, John Baron, etched in the dark stone, but realized the date was too recent. Korinn snapped a photo of the flagstone.

When the friendly Vicar told of ancient records of other Barons he had in his house, I had to decline his offer to examine them. I had been defeated by the clock. I asked for his address; I would be contacting him from Canada. He added the Barons were also his ancestors, thus accounting for having this information so readily at hand. His ancestors were also Barons? That was a coincidence!

"I must confess, Vicar, that I hadn't thought I would find any Barons here so easily. The 1400s was such a long time ago."

"1400s?" Distress and some confusion were evident in his voice. "I am dreadfully sorry, but I just assumed that you meant a more recent period. There are no references to Barons in Mere before the 1600s."

I felt sick. My heart stopped. I had waited five years for this moment and all was lost.

I do not recall our return trip to the hotel room that afternoon. I suddenly just wanted to go home, to have Bob hold me and tell me everything would be all right. But I was not home, Bob was not near, so for Korinn's sake I carried on with the rest of our itinerary.

We saw more sights, toured a crumbling castle, and finally we were on a speeding train to Heathrow and the flight home. I nearly cried for joy when I passed through Customs, and saw *Welcome to Canada* and Bob waiting beyond the barricade.

For the next five days I stayed in bed complaining of jet lag, but I knew that what I was experiencing was a severe letdown. I had been a fool through and through and I was going to have to live with that. Finally, fighting off my mental lethargy, I roused myself and got back into a routine. Sorting through the accumulation of mail, I came across a bulky envelope bearing American postage. Konni had responded to my taped letter with a tape of her own.

"Hi Jewelle, I'll save the small talk for later. I listened to your story . . . how Mom saw you in another life with John Lennon, who was John Baron in Castlemere in the 1400s . . . some of the information isn't quite right. I guess you're wondering why I say this, so I will explain. Over the last few years, as my M.S. has gotten worse, I also seem to have developed psychic abilities. I'll take the liberty of telling you what I see. I see you with a man, John Baron. But it was in the 1600s, not the 1400s, and not in Castlemere, but a place with a name something like *Penhurst* or *Petworth*, in England. There is a hospital connected to where you lived—maybe involving you directly, I don't know. Oh, and one more thing! When I played the song *Jealous Guy*, I was aware of chimes; not in the song itself, but in the background of where you had lived."

Had I heard Konni correctly? I replayed the tape several times before I realized that I had.

Ten

I was so overwhelmed that I scarcely absorbed the remainder of what Konni had to say. My lethargy lifted; my regret about time and energy wasted sloughed off. With this fresh opening, I forgot how my quest had crumbled in Mere. I forgot the tears shed in frustration. All I saw was new hope—hope that I would find Katherine and John after all.

Too excited and impatient to attempt a letter to Konni, I re-wound the tape, and in a few curt sentences asked her to send me absolutely everything she could "see." In the meantime, I would be checking on the places she had given me.

I drove to the post office, and was paying for special delivery when I felt a tap on my shoulder. "Must be a pretty important letter," observed Debbie quizzically. "How was your trip? I want to hear every detail."

I agreed to her suggestion of going for coffee so long as we did not take too long, explaining that I needed to get to the library to find microfiche references. Then I realized how rude I sounded. I hadn't even called her when I arrived home from England, and now I was giving her the brush off.

As soon as the waitress had placed steaming cups of brew before us, Debbie's "Well?" demanded some kind of description of my trip.

Hesitantly, I told her it really was not a success, although as tourists we had enjoyed ourselves. I had not found a St. James in the village of Mere. I told her I did find Barons, even a John Baron, but it was the wrong time period so even finding a Baron, especially a John Baron, was cruel coincidence. Anyway, the gist of it was, I didn't find my John and Katherine from Mere in the 1400s.

Although I assumed Debbie's expression of regret was mechanical, I felt compelled to tell her about Konni's taped message saying that I had lived in England and had known a John Baron, but at a place and time different from those my mother had given me. "So now your sister may be right, when your mother wasn't?" asked Debbie, unsuccessfully hiding a smirk.

I was attempting to point out that I didn't yet know that my mother had been wrong, when she broke in with, "Jesus, Jewelle, why don't you just drop it? What does it matter anyway?"

I wanted to scream. What does it matter? How could she ask that? As my friend, I had hoped Debbie understood me. When I thought about it for a minute, I saw that maybe I was being too hard on her, expecting too much from her. What would I have thought if she had been searching for a past life and paying less attention to this life? Oh course, I would wonder . . . so why wouldn't she? I was running out of the mental energy I needed to analyze this any longer. All I was certain of was, that as long as there was a shred of possibility that Katherine and John had once existed, I would carry on searching no matter what the price.

Looking at my watch and mumbling something about having to go, I tossed some coins on the table and bolted out the café door.

On my way to spend an hour with genealogy, I passed the librarian and found myself wondering what she was thinking about me behind her friendly smile. I went to the English gazetteer to look for Konni's *Penhurst* or *Petworth*. I found a

Penhurst in Sussex, then a Petworth, also in Sussex. I inserted the Sussex fiche into the reader, but neither St. James nor Baron were in either location. Feeling defeated, I was about to leave when the librarian showed me a book which had just been catalogued. It was an illustrated atlas of England which included brief texts about most of the places, large and small. Politely, I agreed to have a look and flipped through the big shiny pages to Petworth.

" . . . Thompson's Hospital built in 1624," I read with surprise. Unless I could find St. James or Baron families living there, what would the mention of a hospital matter?

That night I told Bob of the information from Konni. Shaking his head, he said, "Here we go again, eh?"

"What's that supposed to mean?"

"I'd hoped this trip had gotten this whole thing out of your system. Damn it! How long is this past life-England-Lennon stuff going to go on?"

I couldn't answer. How the hell did I know how long it would go on? For as long as it takes, I thought, but not having the nerve to tell him that. Tucking the children into bed, I felt isolated as I mentally replayed my conversations with Konni, Debbie, and Bob.

What was the matter with me? I thought of John Lennon, or was it John Baron, every day. It wasn't a rock star I constantly thought of, but a memory of someone familiar. Was this normal? Of course not! Was I going crazy? If I was, why hadn't anyone noticed? Or was I just a clever crazy person?

But I could feel this man John Baron. Was he connected to John Lennon? *Was* he John Lennon? God damn it, I would scream to myself. Who are you? Where are you? The only peace I felt was when I thought of John and Katherine, innocent young people, who lived so long ago, oblivious to future lives, oblivious to past lives, simply living in England—a green and quiet England. These feelings were usually short-lived, and again I agonized about the truth.

Two days later Konni phoned.

"Why are you calling in the middle of the day?" I asked. "Did you get my tape? Is something wrong? I found both Penhurst and Petworth in Sussex, England, but there are no St. James or Barons anywhere."

When she could get a word in, Konni told me that if I would be quiet for a minute she would start at the beginning. That morning she had talked to John Baron.

"What? Did you say you talked to him?"

"Well, it was not like you and I are talking . . . more like images."

Konni went on to recount that she had been told about our past lives together in England in the 1600s. "John Baron had come to live with his grandfather in a neighboring town. Your (Katherine's) last name was *James*, not St. James. You were to have been married, but he sickened and died. I saw you as a nurse. I don't know if you were actually nursing him, but I did see you in a hospital. He had a cart or was taken away in a cart. You wore a blue dress when you worked at the hospital . . . the hospital wasn't like a modern one at all . . . it was just a big room or hall. His death was a trauma that has affected both of you in all of your lives since then."

Konni explained that pain eventually surfaces in many different ways. "For you, it surfaced as grief you felt when John Lennon died. While you had never paid him any attention as a Beatle, with the sudden manner of his death, you were shocked into allowing emotions, suppressed for many lifetimes, to surface. It was this sudden and traumatic death in this past life you still need to deal with. If you could remember the Katherine-John story, you could work this past grief out and carry on."

After hearing this I was sobbing my heart out to my sister, long distance from California. "It's so hard . . . I get so lonely . . . I can't talk to people about this . . . it sounds so weird . . . and do you know what is so bloody frustrating? That he had to be John Lennon! The one I loved and lost was just John."

But was John Baron really John Lennon? Or did Lennon just represent a sudden loss; a loss of someone who was loved, loved by so many? Did his death simply symbolize my own losses; loss of youth, loss of Patrick, loss of my dreams?

I was beginning to tire. I knew I had to check on Konni's new information of Katherine being *James*, not St. James. Back at the library, I half-heartedly inserted the Sussex fiche into the reader. My hopes weren't high.

Slowly turning the wheel to James, I gasped. There was Katherine James; in fact there were *two* of them! Born ten years apart! Both in Petworth! Was I one of them? For years I couldn't find one Katherine and now I had to figure out which Katherine was which. Forcing myself to be calm, I remembered what my mother had said so long ago. "Katherine's father was named Robert."

Examining the two Katherines, I first saw *Katherine James, daughter of William, born in 1656, Petworth, Sussex.* Then I saw it . . . there it was! *Katherine James, daughter of Robert James, christened February 24, 1666, Petworth, Sussex.*

While I assumed I would have been the one with the father named Robert, I wanted to get more information. Later I wrote to the Records Office of Sussex and received this reply: " . . . there were several James families in Petworth in the mid 17th Century. From the index of Petworth Marriages and Baptisms, it seems there are at least three Katherine James in Petworth at that period. One was the wife of William James, one the daughter of William James, and one the daughter of Robert James."

I had to see the entry again. Once more my attention was on the Sussex fiche. As I stared, my heart thumped. Just imagine . . . I'm looking at my birth record from three hundred years ago!

Katherine James, christened February 24, 1666, Petworth, Sussex, father, Robert James.

Suddenly I could remember the village of Petworth in the seventeenth century. I could see it in much the same way as I could remember my childhood home in my present life.

I could visualize the narrow, crooked lanes swelled with mud in spring, the stench of open sewers in summer, the beautiful scarlet vines enshrouding stone cottages in autumn. I felt Katherine's presence. She and I were the same soul.

I rushed home and gathered pens and paper. I had to try and capture these memories on paper. As I began to write, my words were hesitant and slow. I had never written a story nor did I have a vivid imagination. However, memories from somewhere flooded into me as the story unfolded. I began to scribble . . . Year 1682 . . .

Konni Frazier

65

Eleven

Katherine's Story

Robert James watched the slow moving lines of seamen, emerging from the ships, with barrels hoisted upon their shoulders. It was the King's Fleet, but he liked to think of it as his since he controlled the goods when they were unloaded. Chichester Harbour was busy with lesser merchants waiting anxiously for their barrels of sugar, silks, oranges, and spices.

As they picked up their goods on the dock, Robert counted, sorted, and collected gold coins from the trade merchants who were about to travel to London. There the goods would filter through the country, everyone adding a gold or silver coin here and copper pence there. Wives and whores stood together on the docks to see their men after months at sea. Children ran about the docks, laughing and shouting. Dogs barked. There was excitement in the air. After months of gray, foggy days, sparsely laid tables and little dance, the sun shone again as spring and the ships arrived together.

Tonight there would be wine flowing, dancing, and full bellies. Even the street urchins would be sated and curled up by a tavern fire, unseen by the merry makers around them.

Robert drank a mug of dark smooth ale, but kept his head

clear and his gold close, for business was not yet over. The next few days would be a repeat of today, counting gold and overseeing the distribution of goods. When his business was finished, he would leave for home in Petworth.

Katherine sat by the fire with her two younger sisters, indulging their childish chatter.

"Tell us about Maggie Hatchett's father," Elizabeth said. "Maggie says if he doesn't get well again, she and her mama could end up in the poorhouse."

Mary asked in her baby voice, "Katie, what's a poorhouse?"

Elizabeth, ignoring Mary, said, "Maggie says her father makes noises that scare her . . . gurgling and choking."

Mary tugged at Katherine's sleeve. "Katie, Lizzie says you empty chamber pots at the hospital, just like Polly does here. Is that true, Katie?"

Their mother had entered the room quietly, and did not hide her disapproval. "Young ladies should not talk so, nor about chamber pots. Katherine does a service to her family by helping the sick, the poor, and the homeless. She will learn humility and gratitude for her station in life by being with those less fortunate."

The girls had heard this speech many times before; they hid their smiles, and did not look at one another.

"Mother, when will Father be home from Chichester?" Katherine asked, not that she was so much interested in her father's return, but more as a way to change the subject.

"When the ships arrive his business has just begun. You should not need to ask. He has done this all the sixteen years of your life."

Although I could remember my life as Katherine, I was having trouble recalling her family clearly. (Months after the story had been written, I checked on microfiche to see if Katherine had had sisters named Mary and Elizabeth. Mary was not on record, but Elizabeth was christened in December, 1670.) For Katherine's parents I had a feeling of respect and fear, but I couldn't imagine a feeling of love. I could remember a servant or someone more like a nanny, a warm woman. I wondered where was she now.

Polly, their old and dear servant, entered the room announcing their evening meal was ready. Mother and three daughters ate a small meal of pork pie and wine, then retired to bed.

Mother came to Katherine's bedchamber as she often did when her husband was away. "Katherine, this year on May Day, you will be attending the ball at the Great Hall. I remember when I was young, there was not as much dancing and merry making. The youth of today have it so much easier," she mused to herself more than to her daughter, who was thinking of the morrow tending the sick and poor, particularly, Mister Hatchett.

Katherine awoke to the patter of rain. Polly brought some cider with bread and cheese to her room. "Here you are, Miss, and you best wear your cloak. The rain is cold even though 'tis spring," she fussed.

As Katherine left the gray stone house, she went through their small garden to the lane. Yesterday, the flowers were opening and the stone bench was warm and inviting. Today, it was cold and wet but she still felt it was beautiful. The rain was heavier now, and she had a mile to walk through the narrow lanes to the hospital. She tried unsuccessfully to avoid puddles, for when the cobblestones ended the Sussex mud began.

Katherine walked head down, only seeing the tips of her leather shoes fighting a battle with the mud. She didn't see the cart or driver until she heard, "My lady, what do I find in the rain?"

She slowly raised her eyes and looked into the bluest eyes

that Katherine, in her small world, had ever seen. "Lady, may I give you shelter and accompany you to your destination?"

Katherine stood there awkwardly. She had never seen this stranger before on the small lanes of Petworth, and he had an air of someone who had seen the world. "Miss?" he questioned.

Wondering if he mocked her, she answered, "Why thank you, Sir." The stranger offered his hand, Katherine gave him hers, and into the cart she went.

Now that Katherine was sitting beside him she felt foolish, and sat there staring at him. His face was handsome but not pretty. His hair was the color of sand, but it was his eyes that held her attention.

"May I introduce myself?" As he smiled, his eyes also smiled. "I am John Baron. I come from Fittleworth where I have recently arrived to live with my grandfather. I have to show my Grandfather Baron that I am worthy enough to be sent to school in Oxford at his expense. He does not part easily with the contents of his coffers, nor his favor, and does not believe men should spend time on books in Latin when there are such things as trade, hunting, and more manly past-times to be learned. But, I am his namesake and for that reason he will indulge me, if I can prove myself worthy." He laughed suddenly. "My lady, I have been prattling on like a fool, and I know not where to escort you."

I could see this blue eyed, sandy headed man as vividly as if I had seen him only yesterday. Someone I had lost track of, but someone I had once known very well.

"To the hospital."

"Are you ill, my lady?"

"Nay I, too, have worthiness to show. By offering my services

69

to the sick, poor, and homeless, I will learn humility, and be grateful for my station in life."

"You say those words as though you have heard them many times."

"Yes," she laughed, "many times."

As they neared the hospital, the sun broke through the gray clouds. John looked up and said, "I'm sure 'tis the same warmth that you bring those wretches in there when you arrive at their bedside . . . a light on a cloudy day."

Katherine suddenly felt warm and she was not sure if it was the sun or this stranger that made her feel this way. She jumped down from the cart.

"Gads, I must hurry."

She realized she had tarried too long, knowing Matron Agnes would be waiting. She gave a small curtsey, while saying, "Goodbye, Sir Baron."

Now it was John's turn to stare. He watched her slight but strong figure hurry away. Katherine's hair fell across her back, thick and dark, bouncing as she ran.

As expected, Matron Agnes was at the other end of the massive hallway, and Katherine could feel her scowl across the distance.

"Miss Katherine James," the matron's voice cut through the air like a chill in winter. "If you are to do service in this hospital, you will arrive before the hour of eight and no later."

"Yes, mistress," she mumbled, "the mud made it very slow going this morn."

She could see Agnes was not convinced, so she hurried off to begin her duties before the matron could say more. As Katherine hurried along she thought of the man with the smiling blue eyes.

I felt uneasy when I wrote of Matron Agnes. I couldn't visualize her features, but her presence made me extremely uncomfortable. I again began to question my sanity as these people from Petworth were becoming real

human beings to me. I feared Agnes. I was fond of Mister Hatchett.
And our servant, Polly, made me feel warm and loved.

"Good morn, Mister Hatchett." Katherine smiled at the dying man as she noticed his color was not so sallow today.

"Ah, my child, I pray to sweet Jesus that these old bones not carry me through another winter."

Katherine tried to look shocked. "Dear Mister Hatchett, you will be back on the docks by the end of summer, fit again, with the sea breeze in your face. Now, no more talk of dying."

"Yes, but . . ." he was interrupted by violent coughing and wheezing.

As Katherine wiped the drool from his face, she felt fortunate to be sixteen years of age and unworried about death. Still, it felt good that it was Spring.

The day went as every other in the hospital. In the morning the patients in her care were fed some bread soaked in milk. Their hands and feet were washed as she tucked their coverlets around them as Polly would Elizabeth and Mary. She tended the fires and found time to gossip with Jane, who was also doing service. Prayers were read to the patients twice a day, although Katherine wondered if anyone was listening. If God existed she had never seen a sign of it, but she never voiced such thoughts.

When the day was done and the night watchers arrived, Katherine and Jane walked through the narrow lanes to their homes. They parted halfway through the village, each going their own direction. As Katherine arrived at the garden gate she sat for a moment on a stone bench thinking about the man from Fittleworth. This morning seemed so long ago.

At the time of writing this, I had no idea what night watchers were. I thought I was simply inventing the word. Years later, I learned that night watchers were at institutions where the patients had the plague or other infectious diseases. The night watchers were there to ensure that no one escaped from the hospital, thus preventing further spread of dreaded diseases.

The week passed with no break in routine except for a free day on Sunday. This day Katherine spent with her family. In the morning they walked to their parish church for services. Elizabeth fidgeted while Mary fell asleep and Mother pretended not to notice, but this was all routine. In the afternoon Katherine sat in the garden doing embroidery while the girls chattered steadily. That evening, as they were about to dine, carriages were heard.

Elizabeth shrieked with delight, "Father's home! Father's home!"

They all rushed to the hall to greet Robert James, who carried delightful looking boxes and packages. He had gifts for everyone; laces and bows for the younger girls, and their mother was pleased with a fashionable new muff and exotic perfume.

Katherine waited patiently and was soon rewarded. A bundle of silk emerged from a carefully wrapped sack. Rich dark green enveloped her as her mother wrapped the fabric around her shoulders.

Katherine's mother gave a look of approval to her husband. "Polly will have this made into a fine gown in time for the May Day Ball."

"Thank you, Mother . . . and Father," Katherine breathed. She knew at sixteen years she would attend the ball, but she had no idea she would have a fine new gown. Now she looked forward to that day immensely. Two weeks seemed a long time to wait.

I seemed to be losing touch with my present surroundings. Physically, I took care of my family, but my mind had become Katherine's mind. My stomach fluttered in anticipation of the upcoming ball that Katherine would attend . . . or was it Jewelle attending? Insomnia became a problem and when I did sleep, I dreamed of Katherine and John dancing . . . always dancing.

The days passed slowly. Katherine longed to be outside in the warm sun and fresh air, picking flowers and watching the new lambs in the fields. As for the poor souls in the hospital, some lay listlessly in their beds, others were demanding and cranky, while some were ready to enter the next world. Mister Hatchett did not talk anymore, though he did smile occasionally. As Katherine cooled a fevered brow or brought flowers to a woman whose days were nearly over, she saw the laughing blue eyes and wondered if John Baron had only been a dream.

May Day arrived. Excitement had been building all week. Older children had been practicing the Maypole Dance. Booths were set up throughout the square, with food and drink for sale. A fortune teller was there but lest she be a witch, only the brave consulted with her. A tooth extractor was there for the entertainment of those who could stomach such scenes. It was not entertaining for the poor wretches with the fat cheeks. Men of labor became knights for the day and some were injured because of their lack of jousting skills. Village girls made eyes at farm boys who returned the compliment.

Katherine arrived as usual at the hospital and until noon she kept to her routine. As she and Jane ate their noon meal of meat pies, Agnes approached them and sternly directed, "If the fires are stoked and the patients are tended to, you may leave for the day. As tomorrow is the Sabbath, I will not expect you 'til Monday morn."

"Thank you, Mistress," they solemnly replied in unison. Agnes bowed her head slightly and left them to continue their meal.

After she left, they started to giggle as Katherine whispered, "Maybe she has a heart after all."

Jane laughed. "But I wouldn't want to say a prayer on it. We had best hurry before her mood changes." And within an hour they were gone.

Katherine hurried home to change out of her plain hospital shift and into a muslin frock. She roamed the square and found her sisters pulling Polly this way and that. Polly was glad to see her.

"Oh Katherine, I finished your gown this morn. Do be home in time to bathe, and we must arrange your hair."

Elizabeth and Mary were tired but happy as they followed the swish of Polly's skirts all the way home. As Katherine came behind them, she remembered being a small girl and the joy of May Day. Now it was the joy of the night she anticipated. The knot in the pit of her stomach grew by the hour. Even though she was excited, she did not know what to expect. 'Soon enough I will know,' she thought.

"Go wait in your chamber, Miss, and I will draw you a bath," Polly ordered.

The metal tub, which was used for special occasions, was filled with steamy water with lavender scent thrown in. Katherine quickly undressed and let the warmth envelope her. She felt calmer now, yet anxious, to see whether her new gown would enhance her or make her look like Lizzie playing in her mother's gowns.

Polly rubbed her skin with a rough cloth until it tingled. Over a small shift, she slipped on the gown. It was plain, rich green with a rounded neck, sleeves that puffed to her elbows, and a skirt that flowed gently from her waist. Polly brushed Katherine's hair until it shone, weaving a tiny string of pearls through the locks which cascaded down her back.

"Katherine, you are beautiful," sighed Polly.

Katherine was afraid to look in the glass, but as she peeked she felt pleased, and yes, she did look beautiful. She stood there for a minute, enjoying the feel of silk against her skin. There was a knock on the door.

"Mother!" Katherine gasped.

"These are for you, my sweet," said her mother, as she lovingly fastened an emerald choker around her daughter's neck. "This belonged to your Grandmother James. The day you were born, she bequeathed it to you, to be given to you on a special day in your sixteenth year."

Unaccustomed to this show of affection, Katherine felt embarrassed. Then her mother abruptly announced, "Your father is waiting. It is time to be on our way."

As they entered the Great Hall, they were announced by the Grand Marshall, who on every other day was known as Willie, the town crier. His voice rang out, "Mister Robert James, Mistress Anne James, and Miss Katherine James!"

They walked through a flowered archway, and were greeted briefly by the Mayor of Petworth. It all happened so quickly, and soon they were mingling with the crowd while other guests were being announced. Katherine recognized nearly everyone as neighbors and friends of her father's. The room was quite full now. Amongst the ladies there was a small hum of chatter. The smell of perfume filled the air. The ladies admired each other's gowns, while secretly thinking her own was the finest. The gentlemen were in green or navy tunics and wore leather shoes with shiny buckles.

Katherine was gazing at the wonder of it all, when she heard the Grand Marshall announce, "John Baron of Fittleworth!"

I could smell the perfume in the air and hear the steady hum of chatter as the Great Hall became increasingly full. There was excitement in the air. I seemed to stand as a spectator, viewing the festive scene before me.

The memory came as easily as if I had only just attended the ball yesterday. When I would pause from writing, looking at my modern surroundings, I felt so very sad.

Katherine could feel the hard and steady thumping of her heart, and as John made his greeting to the mayor, she took in every detail of his being. His light blue shirt with ruffles accented the blue velvet tunic. His knee length pants were met by black leather boots. His sandy hair fell across his forehead, but it was again his eyes that held her attention. They were clear and steady as they gazed about the room. She hoped he would see her, but then felt foolish, for even if he did there was no way to catch his eye with so many lovely ladies in the room.

Robert Philp, tall and gangly, was in front of her asking her to be his partner in a new court jig. He and Katherine had known each other since childhood.

"I'm sorry, Robert, not just yet. I would like to watch the dancing. I may not be able to perform properly . . ." she trailed off.

I could see Robert's red face as clearly as the words on this page. I didn't want to hurt him. He was a friend, but I just couldn't dance with him. Strange as this sounds, three hundred years later, I still feel guilty for the hurt I saw in his eyes.

Her mother, who was standing beside her, whispered sharply, "Katherine!"

"I'm sorry, Robert," Katherine said, pretending not to hear her.

Robert, red faced and flustered, bowed quickly and went in pursuit of a dancing partner elsewhere.

Then Katherine saw John coming across the room. She had not seen him watching her. He, too, had taken in every detail from her rich green gown to her thick, shiny hair. He was standing before her and she had not noticed before how very tall he was.

As John looked down into her eyes, he smiled and asked, "Is this the same girl I found in the rain?"

She smiled, feeling shy, as warmth crept into her face.

Her mother questioned, "Katherine?"

"Ah, Mother and Father, this is John Baron, who resides with his grandfather in Fittleworth. Master Baron rescued me from the rain and mud one day on my route to the hospital."

"I see," her mother replied, but Katherine was not sure what her mother saw.

Her father bowed slightly and said nothing, but Katherine recognized the piercing watchful look in his eyes.

The fiddlers struck up a new melody. John turned to Katherine's parents, saying, "Excuse us, Madam, Sir." He offered Katherine his arm. She laid her hand gingerly on his sleeve as he led her onto the dance floor. As they danced, all she was aware of was the warmth of his body and the firmness of his hands in hers.

"I have missed you, little one. I longed to seek you out, but my grandfather insists that before I think of life's pleasures, I must first learn some of life's lessons."

As they danced, they would gaze at one another solemnly and then would laugh at nothing. Katherine had never felt so happy.

I could see the ballroom as clearly as if I were dancing there right now. The hall was decorated with flowers, the air was warm, everyone was happy, or did they seem to be reflecting my happiness? If I could choose a frozen space in time to live, this is where I would dwell forever. Bob called out to me, asking about dinner. I burst into tears.

The hall was becoming hot from the dancing and the excitement in the air.

John whispered, "Pray, let us escape."

Katherine followed him through the flowered archway outside, where the cool air caressed their faces. They fell silent as they strolled along the stone terrace. The sky was clear. Bright stars shared the night with them. The moon was at its fullest so lanterns were not needed.

"Did you know, my lady, that I am a scholar of the stars?" John looked up to the sky and said, "It is fate that I met you in the rain. See, 'tis written in the stars."

Before Katherine could answer, he put his hand under her chin and gently kissed her.

Katherine sat in her bedchamber gazing out the small window. She was back home in body, but her spirit was still dancing the night away. Why, I am in love, she laughed to herself. Sleep did not come easily that night.

Polly was shaking her. "Miss Katherine, wake up, wake up. There is a young man asking for you. He is waiting in the garden."

"Please tell Mother that I am ill and will not be attending church. Oh, please, Polly," Katherine begged.

Polly started to say something, but the look on the girl's face stopped her. "Oh, very well, run along," she said.

Katherine threw on a light summer dress and wrapped a shawl across her shoulders. John sat on the stone bench, his long legs stretched out lazily in front of him. When he saw her, he jumped up making a mock bow. "Your carriage awaits, my lady."

She laughed. "Where do we go, dear Sir?"

"Ah, you shall see. I have brought bread and cheese, fruit and ale, so we may never return." As he helped her into the cart, she laughed again.

They drove through the winding lanes past the hospital, then over the stone bridge into the country. The grass in the fields was green and wild flowers were everywhere. As the morning sun began to warm them, Katherine marveled at how beautiful the world was.

They stopped beside a small river, and as John unhitched the horse to let him drink and graze freely, Katherine spread a rug and laid out their meal. After they ate, they walked barefoot in the tall grass. When Katherine shrieked at the sight of a small snake, John roared with laughter. He picked her up in his arms and said, "I will always save you from life's many evils."

His laughter was too much for him, for he lost his breath and started coughing. Katherine thumped him gently on his back, and when the color returned to his face, she retorted, "T'is your own fault for laughing at me. You are a lucky man that I was here to save you."

Monday morning arrived, dull and gray. Polly brought Katherine her breakfast as usual and as she ate, the old servant searched her face, but Polly was to be disappointed. The girl offered no account of the day before. As Katherine walked to the hospital, her step was light.

As she entered the hallway, Agnes was waiting. "Miss Katherine, take off your cloak promptly and tend to Mister Hatchett. His hours are few, and until his family arrives he will need someone by his side."

Poor, poor man, she thought. His face was gray and his breathing shallow. She took the weathered old hand in hers and crooned, "Do not give up, Mister Hatchett. Wait for your wife and wait for Maggie." Did his hand grasp hers or was it twitching? She was not sure. They sat as such for an hour until, mercifully, his family arrived.

Agnes approached Misses Hatchett. "Now make your peace,

79

for he will not be here by nightfall." The nurses left them alone, for now his life was in God's hands.

They resumed their duties, stoked the fires, washed down the floor of the hall, and tried to cheer up the other patients who were aware that they could be the next to go. The Vicar arrived and shortly after he left, Mister Hatchett's soul had also departed.

Katherine had watched many patients die and often wondered if the pain they felt was as bad as it looked. She was secretly relieved that she did not have to cry and suffer as she had seen so many others do.

Leaving the hospital for the day, Katherine was subdued and quiet. Walking slowly through the lanes, she said a prayer for Mister Hatchett. As she entered the garden, there on the stone bench sat John. Suddenly she felt like a little girl and rushed to him, putting her hands around his.

Seeing her distress, he asked, "What is it?"

"Oh, 'tis nothing," she sighed, and was glad all was fine in her world.

Summer was a happy time. Katherine served steadily at the hospital and when the stench of the hall grew unbearable or when Agnes frowned with displeasure, she would think of John with his rugged face and sky blue eyes, and all would feel right.

John spent a good part of the summer riding the green countryside around Petworth and, for his grandfather's approval, he became a quick and strong hunter. He also learned the art of sword play, but in his heart his true joy was reading, writing, and the study of the stars. Life for John was good. The nagging chest pain, which he got from time to time, would go away he was sure, when his riding and exercise were finished.

All too soon autumn arrived and the days became less bright; but on Sundays John and Katherine could both escape their duties. It was the first Sunday in October that John arrived in the garden to call for her. "In my ridings with Grandfather, I have found a place that you must see."

Katherine was mildly curious, but as long as she was with John it did not really matter where they went. This day, they started on the road to Chichester. Chichester, however, was not where they were headed. A few miles down the road, John turned the buggy into a narrow path that wandered through a lightly wooded area. He pulled the reins of the horse and they stopped. She looked at him, raising her eyebrows in question. He said, "My love, we shall take a walk."

They walked amongst the thin trees and then across what looked like a farmer's field, when suddenly the earth came to an end. They were standing at the top of a massive set of steep cliffs.

"John," she gasped, "it's beautiful. It's like being on the top of England!"

He smiled. "Everyone should have their own special place in the world and from this time on, this will be our place."

They stood, looking out across the valley of small rolling hills. The golden face of the cliffs melted into the orange and yellow bushes below. They walked along a windy path on the ridge along the top of the cliffs, laughing like children on a spring day.

As they rounded a corner, they nearly collided with a small boy who was skipping and chatting to himself. He was a chubby little thing with long brown curls. John bowed deeply. "Pleased to make your acquaintance, young man."

The boy eyed them suspiciously, then decided to be friendly. He smiled and blurted out, "One day I shall be a knight for the King, the bravest and strongest knight in the land!"

Mildly surprised, John smiled at the boy. "Yes, I believe that you will."

Katherine asked, "What shall we call you, Sir Knight?"

"Jo-Jo," he replied.

John grabbed a bunch of wildflowers from the ground and

with the flowers touched the boy's shoulders, first one side then the other. "I knight thee Sir Jo-Jo of Sussex."

And away the little boy ran, yelling at invisible foe, his curls flying.

Watching the little fellow leave, John said thoughtfully, "We shall name our first child Jo-Jo."

Katherine gulped, "Child, but that would mean . . ."

"Yes, dear Katherine, will you be my wife?"

Katherine felt the world spinning. How she loved the world, and how she would love these cliffs forever, but more than anything, how she loved this man standing there looking down upon her. "Yes, my John," she barely breathed, "I will be your wife."

John smiled and between kissing her lips, he whispered sweet nothings in her ear.

Ten days had passed since John's proposal and she had not seen him. He had not shown up the following Sunday. Maybe he had changed his mind, she thought wildly, and has gone to Oxford or, or . . . ? She was in a panic.

During that time Katherine worked hard at the hospital, not out of dedication, but as a means of passing time. Another Sunday passed with still no sign of John. She sat in the garden and wept. The air was clear and cold, but the only chill she felt was in her heart.

When she arrived at the hospital on Monday morn, Agnes was waiting with the day's instructions. "Good morning, Miss James," she greeted her curtly. "We have a new patient. His grandfather brought him to us in the dead of the night. He says the young man has been burning with fever for a fortnight. He has trouble breathing and has vicious chest pains. What you are to do is apply compresses to his chest, give him plenty to drink, and keep his brow cool."

Katherine went to the kitchen for rags and water, then to find her new patient.

"Sweet Jesus, John!"

There John lay, his hair falling over his forehead in the old familiar way, and when she reached for his hand, it was weak.

"Oh, Katherine, in my dreams I have tried to reach you."

"Shh," she whispered.

"Please make me well, Katherine, for I have a wedding to attend."

"My sweet Sir, you will be as new as a spring lamb in May . . . all you need is rest."

As she applied hot compresses, and looked into John's blue eyes, she tried to believe her own words. She stayed with him late that night, leaving for home only when he was sleeping. The next morning she was up before the sun and gone long before Polly brought her morning meal.

Agnes wasn't in the hall when Katherine arrived. She threw off her cloak and went straight to John.

"Good morning, dear Sir," she smiled, and then the smile froze on her face. His usually clear eyes were glazed, and his face was hot and flushed. She ran for some water which he drank quickly, then still clutching her hand John fell into a deep sleep.

"Katherine," she heard Agnes call, "what are you doing here so early?" Not waiting for an answer, she went on. "No matter, Katherine, the man you are tending is dying, so try to give him comfort."

"Matron Agnes, what do you mean, this man is *dying?*" she hissed. "This man only needs rest. He is young and strong. How can you say he is dying?"

"Miss James," Agnes said slowly, trying to control her impatience, "this man is dying. He has consumption. I will not discuss it further, but to give you proper instructions on how best to care for him."

Katherine listened but did not hear her. When Agnes finished, Katherine walked slowly to the kitchen, her eyes stinging with tears. She felt her whole soul would break into a million pieces. She knew she *had* to be strong. She poured some broth into a cup and carried it back to the hall. John was awake and watching her. He saw her red eyes and asked, "What's amiss?"

"T'is Agnes. We had words. The woman makes me cry in frustration at times. Now drink this broth. It will make you feel better, I promise."

As the days passed, John grew weaker. The days and nights became as one.

One morning, Katherine could see John trying to sit up but he did not have the strength to do so. She put her arm behind his back and slowly sat him up. His uneven breathing returned to normal. Katherine held him as she would a child. Suddenly he straightened up and seemed to possess the strength of the John she once knew. His eyes were piercing as he looked into hers.

"Katherine, I am not a fool. Tell me what the matron says. Am I to be well or will I lie here like an old man, until I shrivel up and die? Curses, Katherine, tell me!"

Her eyes swelled up with tears, and there was no need to answer him. John held her close to him, but what Katherine couldn't see were his own blue eyes clouded with tears.

Suddenly he flung her aside, and started ranting, "Katherine, it's not fair, it's not fair! How can you love me? Look at me, I'm a sick cripple."

Jane, who was carrying some broth, came running and tried to calm him down. He swung his arm, sending the tray clattering to the floor. "Leave me be, you wench!" he screamed. Jane backed up, not knowing what to do.

Katherine mustered all the strength she had ever possessed. "John Baron, *stop*! I love you as much today as I did on the day we met in the rain." Her voice softened, "I'll always love you . . . forever, I'll love you."

84

"Don't you understand?" he pleaded. "I can't leave you to face the world alone."

She whispered, "Of course I understand."

I tried to leave Petworth and concentrate on my present surroundings, but it was no use. I wept as I wrote. I had to go back to John. He was dying. God, don't let him die, I cried, but I knew it was inevitable. I knew I should take a rest from writing. I'd developed a fever, and a deep cough within my chest. Severe pains shot through my stomach.

The doorbell rang. Joanne called to me, "Mom, it's Debbie."

In a daze I went to the door. "Hi," I said feebly, trying to sound normal . . . but what the hell was normal anyway?

"Where have you been hiding?"

"I'm writing a story," I mumbled, "about John and Katherine. I'll call you when I'm finished."

Debbie looked at me with concern, which quickly turned to impatience. "Jewelle, you're living in another world. Can't you see this obsession? You're ruining your life. Can't you understand?"

But John knew that Katherine really did not understand at all.

John's life was leaving him day by day. Katherine would sit with him for hours while he drifted in and out of sleep. Late one night, he opened his eyes and they were clear.

"Katherine," he said, reaching for her hand and smiling faintly, "I promise I'll always be with you. Always remember we are a part of each other . . . remember . . . 'tis in the stars."

Katherine sat for a very long time watching him sleep. Exhausted, she also slept. When she awoke, she saw that she would never again see him smile, feel his touch, or gaze into those sky blue eyes. John was gone.

Time stopped. Weeks, or months, later, Katherine slowly regained her senses. She woke in strange surroundings. She was in an attic room, but where? Only when she peered out a small window, and recognized Aunt Agatha's garden, did she remember that cold, windy night when she had been brought here, kicking and screaming, entrusted to her aunt's care.

Unsteadily, she made it to the door as a coughing fit wracked her body. The door was locked. She started to scream for Aunt Agatha or the family's maid.

Aunt Agatha burst through the door. Her calm voice purred, "Now, now, Katherine, it's time for your medicine."

"I want to see John."

Silly girl, Agatha thought, pining over a young man who could have offered her very little. Agatha knew her brother's family was foolish to let Polly spoil Katherine all these years.

Aunt Agatha hissed, "I've had enough. You know very well your John is gone."

As Katherine had done for weeks she swallowed the laudanum. Agatha wondered if she had given her more than the usual dose. Shrugging her shoulders she left the room, locking the door behind her.

Katherine quickly entered a dream-like state, and drifting she could see John beckoning to her. Then her wasted body became still as her soul rushed in ecstasy to join with his.

At the same moment, Jo-Jo, who was playing in the fields, thought he heard singing in the sky.

Katherine's Story, written in this innocent and child like manner, was channeled to me in seven days. I didn't know from sentence to sentence what would happen next, and in that week I lived (again) in a different century.

After scrawling the last sentence, I collapsed on the couch falling asleep. As I slept, John and Katherine danced.

Twelve

The shrill ring of the telephone woke me. "Your story is nearly right on," Konni blurted, all the way from California.

Startled and sleepy, I managed to respond. "My story? How do you know there is a story?"

"Actually, I didn't, but John did."

"John?"

"Baron. He's been watching you write, and he said you were pretty close to how it all happened. So, you're doing it, Jewelle!"

"Doing what?"

"Remembering."

I was determined that Bob and Debbie read my story. Perhaps it would help them understand. That evening, when the children were asleep, I found Bob stretched out on the couch reading the newspaper. Before he knew what was happening, I had the paper out of his hands and substituted it with *Katherine's Story*. A captive audience, he did not have much choice but to read my literary effort. While he read of Katherine's lost love, I watched his face. For years he had watched helplessly, not understanding the anguish that seemed to consume me. The almost patronizing expression on his face gave way to one of empathy as he reached the final pages. He might not have liked it, but he was beginning to grasp for the first time something of what I was really experiencing.

The next morning, I ventured a first contact with Petworth. I composed a letter of inquiry to the Historical Society of Sussex, requesting information on earlier times in Petworth. I packed up copies of my story for mailing to Konni and my mother. In Mother's I enclosed a note saying, *"I have found my village at last. Petworth is about 50 miles south of London. It's close to a town called Hastlemere—sounds like Castlemere, doesn't it? I found out that Katherine was James, not St. James, and she was born in 1666. You were right about her father's name being Robert. Konni has been helping me. Why didn't you tell me she's psychic? Or did you know? Both you and Konni were aware of chimes when listening to Jealous Guy; interesting, eh? Of course, chimes will be hard to check out."*

After piling the mail near the door, I dialed Debbie's number and invited myself over. Minutes later I was at her door, and before she had a chance to say anything, I shoved a copy of *Katherine's Story* into her hands, ordering her to read it. I would pick it up the next day. Then I was out the door and in my car. Debbie had not uttered a word.

On the drive home the radio belted out *I Saw Her Standing There*, and I slipped into a reverie. The ball held in the Great Hall . . . I would not dance with Robert Philp . . . had Robert actually existed? Was Mister Hatchett real? John's grandfather? Would their names be on record? In the middle of our residential street I made a U-turn and headed for the library.

Within minutes of getting the correct microfiche, I rolled up the surname, Philp, and there staring at me was, *Robert Philp, christened 1664, Petworth, Sussex!* Then I found Hatchett. In my story, Katherine had known her patient only as Mister Hatchett. Here was a *Henry Hatchett* from the right time period.

Since John was not from the Petworth area he would not

appear in the records, but what about his grandfather? In my story I had written, " ... I am John Baron. I live with my grandfather in Fittleworth ... I am his namesake." I slowly advanced the reel. There on the screen was, *John Baron married Susan Elson, Fittleworth, Sussex, 1627*. I could barely read through my tears. A shiver ran down my spine. Could this be John's grandfather?

"Well, what do you think?" I asked, as Debbie poured coffee and handed my story back. "Could you feel Katherine's life?"

"It's a nice little story, but it's only that, Jewelle—a story. Dammit, I have to level with you. You're living in another world. When you first mentioned this "past life" with John Lennon, remember, when we went for lunch? Well, I didn't want to say anything to hurt your feelings, but I thought it was all a little far-fetched. I did try and sympathize with you so you wouldn't get upset, but really, Jewelle, think about it. It's ridiculous! I mean he was John Lennon, and you're a housewife from small-town British Columbia. What is happening to you? I hope you haven't talked to anybody about this. They just might think you're crazy," Debbie concluded with a giggle.

"Debbie," I said, as evenly as I could, "Katherine James is me. She existed. I can feel her presence. I also found her birth record on microfiche. She *is* me! Her father's name was Robert, which is also on record. Mom told me the name Robert (St.) James, years ago. I saw Robert Philp's name on microfiche. He lived in Petworth. Is that a person I completely made up out of the blue? He was born in 1664, two years before Katherine. What are the odds of finding names of people in a small town from three hundred years ago? I saw a John Baron who could have been John's grandfather. I also saw the name Hatchett from that time period and area. Where would I get the name Hatchett? It's a surname that I've never known anyone to have. I didn't find this information out until *after* I'd written about these people. I thought I'd made up the whole thing. How in hell could that happen? This is more than just a story!"

"Coincidence?" Debbie suggested.

"Okay, okay," I countered. "I wonder myself about the John Lennon part, but I believe in John Baron. I feel him. I trust he's here, now. Whether he is John Lennon or connected to him or what, I don't really know, but the rest I'm pretty sure of. I have remembered a past life!"

"Loony tunes, loony tunes," Debbie mocked, in a sing-song voice.

I was stunned. I stood up, and in cold, rasping voice said, *"Bitch."* Neither expecting nor waiting for a reply, I strode out the door.

It was only when I got home that I dissolved into tears. Maybe Debbie was right. Maybe I'd gone completely off the deep end. However, if that were the case, how could the names of people that I had made up just happen to be on record from the 1600s in a tiny village? The odds against that were too high. What about my feelings? I trust my feelings if someone makes me angry or sad. Shouldn't I trust my feelings about the unseen, too?

After I regained my composure, I dialed Debbie's number. Debbie, realizing it was me, assumed her superior manner—I was going to apologize, admit I was silly . . . "No," I said, "I did not call to apologize. I just called to tell you that we can no longer be friends. Good bye, Debbie."

The next morning an envelope arrived, postmarked *Petworth*. Tearing it open, I read, *"Your letter was forwarded to me from the Sussex Historical Society. I am the editor of a small journal we have in Petworth. This journal was established to preserve the character and history of Petworth. I suggest you join our Society, whereby you will be acquainted with Petworth's colorful history. For any further inquiries, please feel free to write to me or, contact our secretary, Mrs. Ros Staker.*" It was signed, *Mr. Peter Jerrome.*

Mr. Jerrome had enclosed a copy of the *Petworth Journal*, and as I stared at the painting of a village square on its cover, I felt strangely at peace. A feeling that was to last for some time to come.

Over the next four years, Konni continued her conversations with John, which she relayed to me through tapes and phone calls. Through these years, not only did I become more acquainted with John's and Katherine's past, I became reacquainted with my sister, Konni.

Our correspondence usually consisted of me sending her Beatles and Lennon songs, which she would do a "reading" on. Usually she picked up on various lifetimes John had, or she could feel the mood he had been in when the song had been written. I knew she had no Beatles music at her house, so I was always amazed at her accuracy. She always knew whether or not John had written part or all of a song. Konni was unable to pick up anything from songs written by Paul McCartney. The idea to send these songs to her first came to me when she had "seen" the same chimes my mother had when listening to *Jealous Guy*. I also verified that they had never discussed this song with each other.

The slow pace of mail service was frustrating and eventually we began calling each other by phone; calls when Konni would have a message from John or I would have a question for him. Day calls weren't cheap, and we both shared the dread of our husbands' wrath over high phone bills! When Konni's bill became so high that the phone company cut her off completely, I cajoled our father into sending her the exact amount of money needed for the bill as a birthday gift.

One day, I asked Konni what she thought of Mom's theory about feelings being the soul's memories of past lives.

"Sure," she said, "I feel more comfortable down here in the States. It just feels right to me . . . not a Canadian feeling to have, I know, so I can relate to feelings."

I said, "There has to be more to this than just feelings, right? I mean, you moved to where it felt right, but most people wouldn't actually try to follow their feelings to the ends of the earth."

Konni laughed. "Yeah, but they try. Travel agencies make a fortune on people who simply *have* to get to a certain country. People who aren't trying to physically get somewhere try and create their past lives with a certain style of clothes, a style of decor in their homes, or it's reflected in their interests and hobbies. Usually, odd traits are just an accumulation of a preferred type of life. The clues to one's past lives are endless."

I thought of Bob's brother, who scraped together money to travel to Jamaica, time and time again. The Jamaica he travelled to wasn't the tourist resorts where exotic drinks and tanned North Americans were the norm. His Jamaica was as primitive as the dirt-floored huts he stayed in, and the fish and breadfruit his diet consisted of. I wondered if he was going back to a previous life, a place he simply had to return to?

Were some of my own traits and oddities reflections of my own past lives? I was the only woman I knew who didn't wear earrings. I disliked shopping. I couldn't keep a garden alive, but I did love wild flowers. I liked horses. I disliked sports. I loved waltzes. The color blue made me feel sad. If I could, I would live on fresh bread and cheese.

The beginnings of my relationship with Bob had started with mystery. Weeks before I had actually met or spoken to him, Bob had seen me in a pub. I was told by a mutual acquaintance that he was interested in me. That didn't prepare me for the surprise of receiving a letter from him, written in Old English, about a stranger arriving at a Baron's Court, and falling in love, at a distance, with a young lady there. Years later, Bob had no explanation for why he'd written the letter in centuries-old prose.

And what of Bob? His dark hair and beard, accompanied by his tall, lanky frame, made him look more like a sailor from days gone by than a modern train engineer. His interest in World War II was, in my opinion, a bit excessive, but who was I to talk about a compulsive interest?

For a time I began to see people in terms of what their past life connections may have been. I saw a neighbour who was not only interested in Tudor times, but her physical appearance resembled someone from a Holbein's portrait. I had a friend whose home not only looked like a 1940s magazine, but her general view of life reflected the same era.

I found this new concept fascinating, but finally I decided to ignore everyone else's lives for a while and just concentrate on John. I asked Konni to see all of John's lives that she could. Over the next few months she had various tidbits for me. She related to me a time when John was a knight from Wales. His name had been George. In another life, also in Wales, he and I had been twins with the surname Llewellyn. I checked out the name Llewellyn on microfiche and after finding hundreds of them decided to stick with John's and Katherine's life in Sussex. (I also did a quick check in an "origin of names" book and discovered that in Wales the name Llewellyn was often shortened to Lewis!)

Konni saw several lives of John's spent as a Jewish man in either New York or London. She told me of a life in London as a well-to-do man. One of his employees was a gardener, who in his most recent life was George Harrison.

I was intrigued with Konni's stories. Some days I was amazed, other days I thought this couldn't all be true. I needed some different verification so as I had done so long ago, I asked Joanne.

93

"Joanne," I said, "Aunt Konni has been telling me about some of John Lennon's past lives. I want to ask you some stuff about it too, okay?"

Joanne, now a teenager, sighed, rolled her eyes and obliged.

I started, "Konni sees that John had been a knight . . ."

She interrupted, "Not a knight in England but a knight in Wales, and his name was George."

All right, all right, I thought. Shortly after my verification from Joanne, I received a sign disguised as a Christmas gift. Bob's sister, who knew absolutely nothing of my search, only that I was an old-and-odd Beatles fan, unknowingly added to my list of strange happenings. Her gift was a poster-sized replica of the *Revolver* album cover, which consisted of a collage of the Beatles in photos, with inserted drawings. I simply stared at the poster. I noticed John in knight's armor, a photo of John looking like an elderly Jewish man, and a photo of John, but his pants had been drawn in plaid. I remembered Joanne saying, when she had first seen a spirit, "Mom, he's wearing plaid."

As the years went by, I began to feel frustrated that I was receiving the answers to my questions through my sister. Not that I didn't appreciate the help. I will always be indebted to her, but I also needed to look to myself for answers. I thought about it for a long time, not knowing how I could actually achieve this.

One day I was so deep in thought I barely noticed a heavy rain against the window. The newspaper, blown from the step, was strewn like tissue all over the lawn. I threw on a raincoat, and dashed out to rescue the paper. It was hopeless. The pieces I could gather were so wet that I took the sodden mess to the garbage can. As I dropped it in, I noticed an advertisement for a *past life regression* by psychic, Laara Bracken. I thought of my earlier psychic reading with Cecilia and how she had seen Patrick's accident, and when I questioned her about John, as to his identity, all she could see was music. Yes, a past life regression would be my next step. Dripping wet, I ran to the phone and made an appointment.

Thirteen

I took a deep breath before I opened the motel door and met Laara. She looked like a youthful fifty-something with soft blonde hair piled high on her head. Her kind face reassured me about being regressed. Her smooth and confident voice dismissed any remaining apprehensions I had about giving her an explanation of what had motivated me to try a regression.

Once I revealed to her that I knew the lifetime I hoped to experience—1600s, in a village called Petworth in Sussex, England—I was able, in ten minutes, to tell her the whole story. It was much easier telling it to this lady than to Bob or Debbie.

The cozy motel room had a rustic country charm, providing a comfortable atmosphere. Laara fluffed up a pillow and motioned me to a nearby couch. She instructed me to relax and, as I lay back and felt the tension leave me, I heard her soft voice beside me. "Have a bell ring in your mind . . . and let the bell bring you to the significant lifetime which involved you with John Baron . . . and let that bell take you back to the village of Petworth, Sussex." Vaguely, I could hear Laara push "play" on a tape recorder.

A car in the parking lot was revving its motor, and a light rain pattered against the window. Slowly the noises melted away as in my mind I approached a village in the centre of rolling green hills. All was silent, except for the barking of a dog.

After a long pause, she continued, *"You are now in the village of Petworth, Sussex. What do you see?"*

I could see buildings that were very close together, but it wasn't very clear.

"Can you get closer? What do you see?"

I saw a square, golden brown and dirty. There were cobblestones, but not modern cobblestones, just rocks put together.

"And the buildings?"

They were dirty, yet a gold color. They were not like the English towns we see now, all painted and pretty.

"What else do you see?"

I saw a dog; it looked a little wild.

"Trees, grass or flowers?"

All I saw was a square with buildings, no greenery, and a lane leading out of the square.

"Take a look down at yourself and tell me what you are wearing."

I was wearing a brownish, golden dress. My hair was long and dark.

"Are you wearing shoes?"

I couldn't tell, my dress hid my feet.

"How old are you?"

"Fifteen."

"Do you have a name?"

"Katherine."

"You are fifteen years old and your name is Katherine? What are you doing in the square?"

I did not know. I did not live in the square. I seemed to be holding a basket. Then I could see more clearly. I seemed to be waiting for someone to come out of one of the houses. I was afraid of the dog because it seemed wild.

"Is there anything in your basket?"

I had bread or buns; little loaves of bread. That was what the dog wanted.

"Where did you get the bread?"

I did not know.

"Look out of Katherine's eyes, down at the basket; where did the bread come from?"

I replied that it came from my aunt. Laara was now addressing me as "Katherine," and I was responding naturally and easily as she continued the questioning.

"Katherine, do you know someone named John Baron?"

I did not.

"All right, you are fifteen. Go ahead five years to when you are twenty."

Suddenly I was dead.

"Katherine, what do you see? Look down at yourself and tell me what you are wearing."

I was buried. I was wearing a light brown dress. I felt no emotion or attachment as I observed my body laying beneath the ground's surface.

Laara realized she had gone beyond Katherine's life.

"Go back to when you are fifteen and you are in Petworth, Sussex and you have a basket of bread. Do you know what year it is, Katherine?"

"1681."

"I'd like you to go ahead one year, to 1682, when you are sixteen. Tell me where you are."

"In the garden."

"What are you doing in the garden?"

I was wandering through the tall flowers.

"Do you know someone named John Baron?"

"Yes, I do."

"We'll move ahead a month. Now, Katherine, tell me where you are."

"On a picnic."

"Who's with you?"

"John. He's standing by a horse . . . its hitched to a plain carriage by a tree . . . he's untying the horse."

"Are there other people around?"

"No."

"He takes care of the horse, and then what happens?"

"We act like children, running in the grass." I giggled at the recollection.

Then, just as quickly, a deep sob wracked my body as I realized that we had not been happy since that afternoon.

"How do you know that?"

I don't know *how* I knew that, I just did.

"You are running about in the grass, acting like children. What else did you do?"

"We talked, laughed, and ate. We made love."

I could feel the sun on our bodies, and smell the earthy odor of the grass. I could smell John! A mixture of fresh air and leather. I could feel John! Rough skin, soft hair.

We had to go back. I had to go home. My parents did not know where I was.

"Stop. Before you go home, I want you to go over to him. You can do this now. Go over to him, take his hands, and look into his eyes. What do you see?"

I saw John's blue eyes, sandy hair, chiselled features, high cheek bones.

"Do you love him?"

"Yes."

"He loves you?"

"Yes."

"How do you know?"

"I know."

"Are you going to be married?"

There were lots of barriers, including parents.

"Why are they against you marrying?"

I did not know, but it was something about John's health. I didn't want to talk about it. I didn't want to face the memory.

"Does John take you home or do you return on your own?"

"We went together. He saw me home. He was not afraid of my parents as I was. Nobody saw us, except perhaps a servant, but she wouldn't say anything."

"Then what happens?"

"He got ill."

"What happens?"

"He died."

"How long after your picnic?"

"It was a few months later. John died from consumption, what we now call tuberculosis."

"Do you blame anyone?"

"The country, for being so wet and cold."

"How do you react to his death?"

I couldn't think straight. Someone seems to be holding me a prisoner, a woman who does not want me to know the truth. Oh, God, I was not sure. After John got ill, my parents used his illness as a convenient way to pressure his grandfather to have him sent away, and I never saw him again. After he was gone, my parents told me he had died.

My parents had promised that my Auntie would take care of me. She would make the hurt go away, but she kept me so drugged my own memories are wrong. I confused my working in the hospital with tending to John. I *did* work in a hospital and John *did* die but have I put the two incidents together?

I just don't know the truth. *Now I'm a prisoner in my own room.*

I start gasping, "Auntie, Auntie, no more medicine!"

I tried to visualize Auntie, and then, Debbie! I saw Debbie in the room with my Aunt Agatha. Debbie was called Rachel.

Rachel had been hiding, and when my Auntie left she gave me more medicine. I tried to tell her that I had already had my medicine, but I could not speak. I could not think. Everything was fuzzy. I was dying. I could see John waiting for me.

Laara said, calmly yet firm, "*Jewelle, Jewelle. I want you to leave the situation, and go back to the time when you and John are at the picnic. I would like you to picture a white light wrapping itself around both of you. You do not have to go through that pain again. The same white light is now being sent to the picnic area and is healing all from that moment to this moment. Let all the old grief turn to loving energy, and know that the rift between you and your soul mate has now been healed. See yourself as whole, both male and female, John and Jewelle.*"

I was back in the room with Laara, lying on the beige couch with the pillow under my head. I heard the tape recorder click to a stop. I was surprised to find my cheeks were damp. Although I was dizzy as I sat up, my thinking was crystal clear. I had to go home, to Petworth. I had to go home.

Fourteen

My view of Katherine's life had changed. When writing Katherine's story, I had a bittersweet remembrance of her time with John. However, the regression took my memories and made me fully feel her life in the 1600s. Through Katherine's eyes I was aware of having no concept of the world outside of Petworth. I was surprised at how my perception of life three hundred years ago had changed by experiencing it. Petworth in the 1600s was drab and dirty, people worked hard and played hard, and their lives were short and futures uncertain. I was aware that Katherine accepted her primitive conditions in the same way we accept the many flaws of living in the twenty-first century.

I had reached a crossroad. To complete my search once and for all, I would have to go back to England. I couldn't continue chasing shadows. I needed to know whether I had lived in this Sussex town, whether I had known John, and a hundred other details.

This was my final decision. If I came to a dead end as I had in Mere, I would put the whole thing away knowing I'd experienced the ultimate delusion. If I succeeded, I would write a book for those like-minded people I knew were out there. If I could reach one person who may be experiencing what I have, my purpose would have been accomplished.

I dropped hints to Bob that maybe another trip overseas was in order, saying I needed to check out Katherine's and John's past lives once more. Bob hinted in return that if I earned the money, that would be a good place to start!

September, 1989, I started a part-time job at the elementary school my youngest daughter, Kristy, attended. Every day as I walked to school, I knew I was one step closer to finding my answers. Other days, when I wondered if there *were* any answers, my mood would lift by viewing the world through the innocent eyes of young children.

I began to prepare for the last mile of my search. I had learned from my experience at Mere. My only focus in England would have to be Petworth and I would have to stay there, not just drop in casually for an afternoon.

I wrote to Peter Jerrome (chairman of the historical magazine, *Petworth Journal*) under the guise of researching the James family in the 1600s.

Through my genealogy group, I found the address for the Sussex Records Office. Not only did I inquire about Katherine James, but about other details of *Katherine's Story*. I felt ridiculous trying to find the right words. How could I ask whether laudanum was abused by indifferent aunts? Or how many people they had on record who fell in love at balls held in a Great Hall? Or was there even a Great Hall or . . . or? Finally I composed questions I hoped sounded professional.

Throughout this time I continued my many phone calls to California. My sister insisted that John would like me to try communicating with him myself. How was I supposed to do that?

Konni said, "Be calm, lie down in a quiet room, close your eyes, and he will be with you."

I tried. I would get a vague impression of him but was it my imagination? Sometimes I would drift off to sleep, dreaming that we were dancing, but aren't dreams just another way of imagining, or are they? One day I saw him vividly, and I didn't hesitate to wonder if this was real. I visualized myself leaving my body. My spirit joined with his, as we looked down on planet Earth. He took my hand and said, "Would you like to see Petworth? I'll take you there."

As we approached the English town, I could see a soft pinkish glow in the distance. As we came closer, my attention focused on a church spire, glowing in the same pink hue, that rose proudly and protectively above Petworth. Then all was gone, and I was back on my bed. Had I been seeing things? Why was everything all pink? I decided my imagination was getting better and better all the time!

Months later, I read this tidbit in an English book on various villages in Sussex. I realized I could only accept that there is so much more to this world than I'll ever begin to understand.

> "The church in Petworth, on the highest point in town, is an architectural mixture of many ages. There is no trace of the Saxon church the Norman registers noted, but there are echoes of the thirteenth and fourteenth centuries. What makes the greatest impact on your vision is the strong tower. The stone base is medieval. Sir Charles Barry added the top part of the pinkish-red brick in the early nineteenth century, and he also replaced the faltering spire with a new one which became a landmark, easily picked out above the surrounding hills, valleys, woodlands, and meadows. But this too, weakened, became a danger and was taken down in 1947."

Pinkish-red brick? The spire taken down in 1947? What did this mean? I'd heard of the concept of "no time" and I suspected this was some proof of that theory. Again, I simply had to accept that my visualizing this pink tower couldn't have been my imagination.

Then one day Peter Jerrome's letter arrived. It said the James family had been a large and scattered one through this part of Sussex in the 1600s. He had enclosed a book titled, *Cloakbag and Common Purse*, about a *"William James, who in the late 1500s in Petworth, was a tenant's leader in a court battle with Henry Percy, 9th Earl of Northumberland, who had allegedly illegally enclosed this tenant's copyhold land in Petworth."*

It was interesting that a member of the James family was referred to as a "tantalizing figure in Petworth's history," and I wondered exactly what relation he may have been to Katherine. I was also interested to note the author of the book was Peter Jerrome himself!

The next few months brought bits and pieces of information from the Records Office. They were: *In the 1600s there was a Great Hall, in which many entertainments would take place . . . this Hall no longer exists, Petworth House having been rebuilt. The only hospital in Petworth in the 1600s was Thompson's Hospital, founded in 1624 for the maintenance of twelve poor persons. There would be a matron. There are no lists of inmates before the 19th Century.*

I not only learned that the spelling of personal names wasn't yet standardized, but the name of Petworth had been varied through the centuries, with the first name coming from a Saxon derivative, *Pytta's enclosure*. The Norman *Domesday Book* mentions *Peterode*. In 1205, *Peiteworth*. *Putworth* in King Edward I's time, *Petteworth* in Medieval times, and *Pettewoorth* in Henry VIII's time.

I learned, too, that a manor had always been the centre point of Petworth, with the Great House first being mentioned in the year 791. A thousand years later, Petworth House was still the focal point in Petworth. This boggled my mind as I looked around at my own surroundings in B.C. which had barely existed a hundred years ago.

I was absolutely fascinated by the history of this town. I felt I couldn't wait any longer to try and find answers. Although I had been working and saving money, I didn't have nearly enough money saved to travel to England, but I simply had to go.

I approached Bob, expecting an argument. He surprised me by looking at me intently. "You really have to go, don't you?"

Before I could reply, he said, "Go . . . do it, get it over with." Before he could change his mind, I phoned the travel agency and booked a flight in September. My Visa bill was my second guilt trip. My first was leaving Bob alone once more, as I set off again to try and solve my past life losses.

Remembering Peter Jerrome's advice to write to the secretary of the *Petworth Journal* if I needed more information, I did just that. I asked her to please send me tourist information. A few weeks later, Mrs. Staker not only sent me a town guide but also an invitation to drop in for coffee when I arrived.

I browsed through the small guide at the listings of bed-and-breakfasts establishments, when one caught my eye—*Minutes from town, a Tudor town house* . . . I immediately wrote, asking for a reservation in the last week of September.

I was days away from my departure. I was excited and nervous; everything was at stake. This would be the trip that would decide my fate, whether I would give up the whole search or carry it to the end.

My bags were packed and everything was in order. Minutes before leaving the house, Konni phoned. "Hi, I'm glad I caught you before you left. John just told me to remind you of the bluebells. He says you loved them. They grow wild . . . fields of them in the woods . . . maybe you'll see them."

"Bluebells," I laughed. "Okay, I'll add them to my list."

I arrived at Gatwick Airport on a warm and sunny afternoon in September, 1990. I planned to follow the route I had planned for months; take a train from the airport to Pulborough, the nearest train station to Petworth; take a cab the last five miles to Petworth. The whole trip wouldn't take more than an hour.

Tears came to my eyes as we sped south through the rolling green Sussex countryside, sprinkled with majestic oak trees and grazing sheep. The scenery was exactly as I had remembered it when writing *Katherine's Story*. I knew I was nearly home.

I wiped my eyes and gathered my bags as we pulled into Pulborough station. The train door wouldn't open! There was no conductor in sight as I tugged and pushed at the door.

"God damn it," I muttered, panic setting in. Once again the fast train was pulling out of the station. Feeling like a fool, I approached the only other passenger, a woman about my age. My voice was quivering. I was shaking. "I couldn't get the door open; where is the next station?"

"Amberly. The doors are child proof. You have to put your hand through the window and open it from the outside."

A variety of unkind thoughts, directed at Britrail, sped through my head as I thanked the woman who helped me with the door at the next stop.

The train stopped only long enough for me to quickly alight onto a platform, then swished out of sight. I looked around, but there was not a person in sight at the seemingly abandoned station. The dark red building, decorated with an abundance of flower boxes, sat shimmering in the sun. I looked through the station's windows and tried the doors. Everything was locked. A sign on the door said it opened at 5:00. 'Great,' I thought, 'it is only 2:00.' Dejectedly I limped along, with heavy luggage in tow, across an overhead footpath which took me to the platform on the opposite side of the tracks. I would just have to wait for a train going back to Pulborough.

I sat on a bench, my only company a bee that droned around a nearby flower box. Total exhaustion, and the ludicrous situation I was in, was too much for me and I began sobbing.

Drained, I wiped away my tears and then stared in disbelief. I hadn't noticed that directly in front of me, back across the train tracks, were massive white chalk cliffs. I stood in *awe*. White cliffs several feet away! I remembered the very first time my Mom had told me about John and Katherine. I recalled her words, "I see white cliffs, fog, and lush green grass." For a long time I sat alone in the presence of the stark white cliffs, and I knew that I'd missed my train station for the purpose of simply arriving at these cliffs.

Hoisting my bags to the most comfortable position possible, I left, walking down a short lane. I came to a beautiful stone house with a massive garden overflowing with color. An elderly lady answered the door, and I had to control my tears. "Hi, I have just arrived from Canada. I got off at the wrong station, and I'm trying to get to Petworth. Could you please call me a cab?" Hesitantly, the woman asked me to wait a minute as she called to her husband. I pretended not to notice their obvious suspicion as I repeated my problem.

After a few moments he offered, "I will drive you to Petworth."

I sat back and relaxed as we turned off the highway to a smaller road which had a sign indicating Petworth, 5 miles. Minutes later, the elderly gentleman came to a stop in front of Grange House. I thanked him for his kindness, and with a cheery "good luck" he left me on the sidewalk.

Fifteen

The white Georgian-faced house, which was to be my bed-and-breakfast lodgings, was smaller than I had expected. Responding to my rap on the door, a pretty young woman greeted me warmly and invited me into the sitting room.

A grand rustic fireplace dominated the tiny room, dwarfing the stuffed sofa and chairs. What caught my attention was the pram sitting in the middle of the room. "My daughter . . . she's seven weeks old," said the proud mother. "Would you like a cup of coffee or tea?"

As I sat in the cozy kitchen, drinking tea and chatting with my hostess, I felt comfortable and so glad I had finally arrived in Petworth.

To her query about visiting my family, I explained, "No, I do not have family here but I'm doing family research. I'm into genealogy and tracing my family tree." At her polite, but disinterested response, I knew we had exhausted the conversation.

I gulped down my tea and suggested that I would like to settle into my room. Grabbing one of my bags, my hostess led the way up the stairs. I was aware of the faint aroma of potpourri and furniture polish. The staircase which led from the sitting room was steep and narrow, typical of ancient houses. The landlady announced that she would put me in the top attic room so the baby wouldn't disturb me.

Oddly, a sense of foreboding suddenly came over me when we started the ascent of the second flight of stairs. Nearing the top, the stairs took a sharp turn. I felt an icy chill run through my body. I experienced a reluctance to go any further but, nevertheless, followed the landlady into the room which was to be home for the following week. I was told to watch my head as we entered the attic room. My hostess departed after inviting me to have a bath if I wished. I sat down on the huge wooden-framed bed and looked around the room. It had thick beams supporting the slanted ceiling. I wondered if the wrought iron chandelier was salvaged from a dungeon somewhere. The long, narrow window above my head provided a beautiful view of Petworth House and the surrounding town in the distance. I felt silly about my momentary sense of panic and was glad my hostess had not detected it. Guessing that fatigue was to blame, I chose to have the suggested hot bath. After a long soak, I donned jeans and a sweater, announced that I was off to walk around Petworth, and set out to see all I could.

Narrow, ancient lanes wound this way and that. Traces of Medieval times were everywhere. Quaint stone cottages had tiny garden plots filled with colorful flowers. There were lace curtains adorning most windows, and milk bottles waiting on door steps. The lanes, like erratic spokes in a wheel, converged on a large square where the many shops vied for every available bit of frontage. Dodging the traffic that pinwheeled about me, I cut across the square and entered a particularly narrow alley that twisted into a much smaller square, only paces from the first.

I stood rooted to the spot. This was the square I had seen in my regression. It was here I had been Katherine, holding a basket of bread. The buildings around, my dress, the cobblestones . . . all the same golden, brown color. I had wondered why the scene had been all one hue. Now, as I looked about me, I had no doubt this was the same square. A brass sign hanging from a corner post read, *Golden Square.* Had I been seeing things in a kind of symbolic color in the regression the same way I had seen Petworth in a pink hue when looking at the old church tower? An interesting concept. One I didn't understand, but a concept that had definitely happened to me twice.

On the opposite side of the square was an arrow pointing to Petworth House. Crossing the square, I found myself at the huge wooden door at the front entrance. I followed a small crowd of people inside. Barely aware of the Van Dycks and Turners, and the other decor, I suddenly felt disoriented and sought refuge at a nearby bench, and railed, "What in hell am I doing here? What kind of idiot am I, coming all this way and hoping to find some stupid clue? I was through all of this before at Mere."

I sat on the bench for what seemed like a long time, staring into space. Finally, I forced myself to move and found myself in a long, narrow corridor with a low ceiling. The walls were covered with many black plaques. I was aware of feeling a strange mixture of calm and apprehension. I was most certainly reacting intuitively to these surroundings. I hurried through the corridor and out into the late afternoon sun. I stood for a while, staring back at the magnificent building, feeling nothing familiar about the stone exterior. I was almost relieved.

I strolled through the manicured lawns and rounding the corner of Petworth House, I saw St. Mary's Church a stone's throw away. Here was the same church I'd seen on my "trip" with John, not at a distance this time, but right in front of me. I quickly entered the quiet churchyard. With growing excitement, I approached the enormous wooden door and pushed it open.

The only light came filtered through stained glass windows, casting odd shadows on tattered and worn pew cushions. On one wall were plaques commemorating people from days gone by. No matter how hard I tried, I could not feel any link with the cold, dark place. As I was about to leave, I was startled by a tall thin woman sliding past me carrying a pile of papers. I called to her, explaining that I was doing research on various old Petworth families. I asked to see the church records from the 1600s, and told her I wished to see the Vicar if he was in.

"I'm sorry," she replied, in a clipped manner, "the Vicar is not in today. And, anyway, there are no records kept here, the original records are much too valuable to just let anybody look at, aren't they? You'll have to go to the Records Office in Chichester to look at anything from this parish."

I wandered slowly around the churchyard, observing ancient and decaying tombstones. Modern Petworth was hidden from view by lush green oak trees, and as I looked at the headstones I wondered if any of the James family was buried here, or John, or me? Was I looking at my own grave and not knowing it? *Four years later, my last verification was a letter received from the Records Office stating that Katherine James, daughter of Robert James, was buried in St. Mary's churchyard in 1683! Most of the tombstones were illegible but, indeed, I had been looking at my very own burial site.*

I sat in the church garden, mulling things over until the sun began to set and the air chilled. Throughout my stay I would often wander through the cemetery that surrounded the church and, for brief seconds at a time, I could nearly touch ghosts from the past.

I followed ancient Lombard Street, a cobblestone lane, back to Market Square, to a Tudor tea shop and ordered tea and fruitcake. I consulted my notebook, which contained a list of places I wanted to see. However, at that moment, it was human contact I needed. I thought of Mrs. Staker who had sent me tourist information about Petworth and who had invited me to drop in for coffee. Not used to dropping in on people unannounced, I decided to go before I lost my nerve. I paid for the tea and asked directions to #29 Green Lane.

The semi-detached house looked cozy and inviting, but I found myself wondering, as I knocked on the door, whether Mrs. Staker would be strange, or worse, rich and eccentric! Answering the door was a robust woman, dressed in a traditional English gray tweed skirt accented by a cream colored blouse. I hesitantly introduced myself, saying I had just arrived from Canada, and reminded her of the pamphlets she had sent. Her conservative dress, however, was not reflected in her manner. Her twinkling blue eyes and wide smile warmly greeted me as she invited me in, offering to make coffee.

Mrs. Staker looked at me thoughtfully. "This is the strangest thing. Just this morning I wondered when Mrs. Lewis would arrive. Funny, and here you are."

She had me sit at an oval table covered with a crisp linen cloth, and disappeared into the kitchen for coffee. I immediately felt at home. From the kitchen, my hostess remarked, "I just can't get over thinking about you only this morning. I had pictured you as being about seventy, very rich, the kind of woman who travels a lot dabbling in different curiosities. So what exactly are you doing in Petworth?"

Asking her to please call me "Jewelle," I launched into my story. "I am here because I am sure that I lived another life in Petworth, three hundred years ago. I am trying to check that out. Coming to Petworth is the last stage of my search." Within minutes, I had poured out the whole story to this English lady who already seemed like a friend. However, I omitted my suspicions about being connected to John Lennon.

Mrs. Staker responded by saying it was quite a story and she knew just the people I should meet, starting with Peter Jerrome of the *Petworth Society*. "Yes," I told her, "his was one of the names on my list." She added Jumbo Taylor, a nice chap, who probably knew more about Petworth history than anyone.

I couldn't believe the interest this woman was taking in me, as she talked about the different people who could help. I had the strange feeling that all of this had been staged and all I had to do was go along with the script. I asked her if she had time to do all this for me. She exclaimed, "Gads, yes! This kind of thing doesn't happen every day. So what did you do today, then?"

I told her about my rather weird first day, how I had familiar feelings about Golden Square, the corridor at Petworth House, and the churchyard. "I would start to choke up at nearly every corner. I'm sure that half the population has noticed this foreign woman blubbering her way across town. Mrs. Staker, I'm so glad I have met you!"

"Mrs. Staker! Blimey, please call me Ros."

Ros offered to walk me back to my lodgings as the street was very dark. The winding lane was a little eerie, being lit only by a pale moon, so the company was appreciated. It was a pleasant evening, and with the day's roar of traffic through the village silenced, the only sound was our chatter.

As we neared my bed and breakfast, I told Ros that I had been using two ways of putting my story together—first getting information from psychics and then trying to check it out factually with proof. I was in Petworth in order to get some black and white proof.

"Well, I don't know about that," Ros said, "but I know of a psychic who is very good. She lives in Tillington, a mile or so away from here." At my eager reaction, she promised to see what she could do about arranging a meeting. At that, we said good night and I entered my bed and breakfast.

The warmth and aroma of the roaring fire in the fireplace

followed me up the first flight of stairs enroute to my attic room. However, on the second flight, I felt a cold chill. The feeling slowly subsided after settling into my room. I was out of my clothes quickly. Taking a white flannel nightgown from my bag, I slowly let it fall over my head. I imagined myself having thick, dark hair cascading down my back, and I recall thinking that exhaustion does funny things to one's mind. I fell into bed and was instantly asleep.

Golden Square, Petworth (PHOTO: JOANNE ALARIC)

Sixteen

I woke to a still and quiet room. Stretching lazily, I groped for my watch. It was nearly noon! As I took a quick bath, I mentally planned my day. After applying make-up and dressing for action, I flew down both flights of stairs.

In the kitchen, my hostess greeted me with, "Oh, good morning, or should I say, good afternoon?" Still feeling the effects of jet lag, I declined breakfast, asking only for juice.

Serving me a glass of cold orange juice, she said, "A lady named Ros Staker was here this morning. She left a message for you to meet her at her work place at 12:30. She left a map. It's a brick building between Market Square and Golden Square and has a sign: *Dr. Morrow – Dentist.*"

12:30! That was minutes away! I gulped down the juice, thanked my landlady, and dashed out the door.

I was aware of blue skies and warm air as I walked swiftly along the lanes toward the large square. I found the red brick building and as I entered, I encountered Ros wearing a white medical coat and a broad smile. "Your landlady said you were crashed out this morning. Jewelle, I would like you to meet Ann. We work together. We've finished up here for the day, so I thought we could all have lunch together. There's a pub just around the corner."

Ann was an attractive blonde woman in her forties. As she shed her medical coat, I noticed that, unlike Ros' more conservative apparel of tweed and wool, Ann could pass for an American, dressed in jeans and a bright sweatshirt.

I could tell that these women were more than coworkers. They were outgoing and shared a friendly sparkle and wit, which quickly made me feel as comfortable with Ann as I had meeting Ros. To my relief, because I was getting tired of repeating myself, Ros had already told Ann my story.

The pub was dark and quiet, with small oval tables facing an unlit fireplace. The few patrons spoke no louder than whispers.

Seeing no sign of a waitress, Ros strode up to the bar to see about lunch. Ann and I chose a table and sat down.

"So, Jewelle, you've come all this way to check this out? Fascinating. My daughter would be interested in your story. She has "a gift," as we call it. When she was young she would often be frightened by spirits who would approach her, but now she can talk to spirits as easily as I am talking to you. She is quite private about it and only talks about her experiences within our family. I am sure she would be interested in you."

I couldn't believe it! Ros, last night, telling me of a psychic who lived close by, and now Ann telling me of her daughter, Becky, who has a psychic "gift."

Ros triumphantly returned, bearing pub lunches for all. As she sat down, she informed me that she had made arrangements for us to meet the psychic that evening. "I told Pet briefly why you are here and . . ."

"Her name is Pet, as in Petworth?"

"Well, no, actually it's Petula, and she's looking forward to meeting you."

Petula lived in a neighbouring village, Tillington, but thought it better to see me in Petworth since that was where I felt I had lived. We were to meet at the dentist's office where

Ann and Ros worked, and since the building dated from the 1600s Pet felt it might have vibrations from that time. I wondered if Ann was to be there. She admitted she would be interested, if I didn't mind. I felt it natural that both she and Ros be there, and said so.

As we sat and chatted, I felt a deep sense of belonging. Taking a deep breath, I stated that I should tell them something more before we saw the psychic that evening. When I indicated the fellow I was involved with in the 1600s might be the same soul as John Lennon, Ros and Ann glanced quickly at each other. Suddenly I was scared they thought I might be a nut case.

"You know," Ann said, "I'm sure Paul McCartney has a home in Sussex."

Was she making fun of me? I added, emphatically, that Paul McCartney had absolutely nothing to do with my story. Suddenly, we all laughed at the thought, dissolving any remaining tension I had felt.

I went on to tell them of how, for four years after John Lennon was killed, I had been in a state of perpetual grief. Grieving for someone I had never met! If I had been a fan, it might have made some sense, but even fans don't think of someone every single day. Finally, when I couldn't stand it any longer, I had asked a psychic if there was any reason for this grief. To make a long story short, I got the names and dates of ancient people connected with me and here I was in Petworth. I still had one big question I hadn't voiced aloud—are/were John Baron and John Lennon one and the same soul, or did John Lennon's death merely trigger some memory?

"Well," said Ros, finishing her lunch, "maybe Pet can answer some of your questions tonight. I'm glad I didn't know of the John Lennon part when I talked to her. This way she can pick up whatever there is, with no preconceived ideas. In an hour, though, I've also arranged a visit with Peter Jerrome, the editor of the *Petworth Society Journal*."

Ann and Ros chatted on about local gossip, and I felt as though I had always sat there in the Angel Pub enjoying the company of old friends.

As we left the dark pub, back out into the bright sunshine, Ann suggested that we go to the cemetery at the end of the lane and look for ancient names. From the lane, we entered a small alley leading to an unkept cemetery. We found ourselves knee-high in brittle grass, which caught at our feet and made the headstones barely visible. It was evident from the inscriptions that we were able to uncover that this burial ground dated only from the 1800s.

We continued walking down the alley. Without warning, the village abruptly ended. I saw that we stood on a slight ridge overlooking a valley of soft green grass shimmering in the afternoon sun. Never had I seen a more beautiful sight. I later learned that this shimmering valley is called Round the Hills. As we silently made our way single file down the path, I became aware that there was something familiar in the distance and asked the others if it was a road.

We focused our attention on what was but a faint trace of a road which branched off the path on which we stood and wound its way across the valley and disappeared on the opposite side. Ros ventured that it was likely the ancient, long-abandoned road to Fittleworth. Before us, our path looped through a wooded area and back into the village. I felt compelled to glance back over my shoulder at the ancient route. As Ros and Ann chatted, I drifted along in their wake, lost in thought.

Noticing my silence, Ros inquired whether I was nervous about meeting Pet. "No," I said slowly, "I'm just so confused about the familiar feelings I had when seeing the corridor in Petworth House, and St. Mary's churchyard. The sight of the valley and its ancient road also gave me these mixed emotions." Wistfully, Ros commented that the valley probably looked the same now as it did three hundred years ago.

Then, suddenly aware of the time, Ros said good bye to Ann and steered me in the direction of Peter Jerrome's home. Ann went around the corner and disappeared into one of the many lanes off Market Square, while Ros and I approached the doorway of a small shop.

A tinkling bell announced our entry. A petite woman behind a counter looked up and responded to Ros' greetings and my introduction. Marian indicated she anticipated our visit, but was a bit puzzled, as was Peter, as to why we wanted to talk to him. She locked the shop door. "I do say, though, I am quite intrigued. Please, do come in."

Marian led us up a short flight of stairs, through a maze of unusually shaped rooms, into a small, chilly sitting room. She invited us to sit down and went to inform Mr. Jerrome that we had arrived. I chose a stuffed chair opposite a ground-level window that looked out on a garden bursting with color. In the quiet room, as Ros and I waited, I heard the ticking of an unseen clock.

Peter Jerrome entered. He was a tall, spare man in his fifties, inclining his head to one side, betraying an inquisitive nature. Although he had the reserved, polite manner characteristic of English men, I sensed a doubtfulness in his expression as Ros introduced us. "Ros tells me that you believe you lived in Petworth, in another life, you say?"

At Ros' urging, I started into my story. I told the whole story, detail by detail, trying to stick with the highlights of my search. Marian had served tea in dainty china and was sitting, listening, wide-eyed as I concluded, ". . . so I have come to Petworth to see what I can learn of these people and places, Katherine James and others."

Peter acknowledged the research difficulty since the 1600s were such a remote time and asked for the names. I listed Katherine James, her father Robert James, a Mister Hatchett, Robert Philp, and a John Baron from Fittleworth.

Peter zeroed in on Robert Philp. "Robert Philp, you say? Born when?"

"1664."

"Well," Peter smiled for the first time, "this is his house in which we are sitting."

Ros' exclamation of surprise equalled my own as I realized that I was looking at my first tangible connection with Katherine. Then, in a split second, I saw my seventeenth century friend. Robert Philp was Peter Jerrome!

"What does your husband think of all this, Mrs. Lewis?"

Typical male question! Keeping a straight face, I told Peter of Bob's skepticism, which was natural for someone of his pragmatic nature, and that his skepticism had started to weaken somewhat as "proof" of the existence of these people started to emerge.

That elicited little response from Peter. He rose from his chair, said that it was very nice meeting me, and that he really had to get back to his afternoon's work. I was not surprised at the abrupt end to our meeting, and watched with a feeling of fondness as this old friend departed the room, waving off our thanks. Marian saw us to the door. As she unlocked the door, she said, "I'm afraid Peter is a little skeptical about these things, but I found your story to be just delightful." The little bell tinkled at our departure.

We were standing at the edge of the square, analyzing what we had just experienced. Ros voiced her opinion that it was hard to tell what Peter was thinking. She suggested going to her place for tea before we visited Pet. I assured her that, although I had put a lot of hope on his being the one who would answer all my questions, Peter had given me an unexpected piece of information regarding Robert Philp's house. However, I didn't say that not only had I seen Robert Philp's house, but I suspected that I had also seen Robert Philp!

Ancient Lombard Street looking towards St. Mary's Church (PHOTO: JOANNE ALARIC)

Seventeen

We sat in Ros' cozy dining room, drinking tea and nibbling biscuits. I asked, "Tell me about Pet. I'm picturing an older woman with a shawl and heavy jewellery."

Ros threw her head back as she laughingly refuted that image. "Pet is just an ordinary person—thirty, married with kids, talkative, observant. I sometimes forget she's doing a reading. Unexpectedly, she will say something such as seeing a spirit beside me or something connected to me."

I admitted a growing apprehension about seeing Pet, and how I felt that way every time I had consulted a psychic. I was always worried about what I would be told, yet, I was still willing to take that chance.

Unlike this morning, I studied the ancient red brick building as we approached the dentist's office. I was fascinated by the idea that Katherine would have passed this very building many times in her lifetime.

Ann and Pet were waiting for us in the receptionist's room. I suddenly felt shy as Ros introduced me to the tall, graceful woman with a long strawberry-blonde ponytail. She barely looked twenty. "Thanks for seeing me," I said.

Completely putting me at ease, she said warmly, "Really, it's my pleasure."

We all sat in big, overstuffed chairs in the dentist's waiting room and quickly the mood changed. Pet took a deep breath and looked intently at me. *"I'm getting strong vibrations relating to you. I see you a very long time ago in Petworth, as a young girl. You are petite, and you have long, dark hair. Your father, a merchant, though not of their class, is nevertheless accepted by the gentry. There is an elderly aunt, either in your home or nearby. You have met a young man, with whom you are falling in love. He is from an aristocratic family, but socializes with your family. He is physically frail, he is often ill, his future is unclear. Not only physically frail, he's thought of as being slightly mad. He isn't mad, he's just different, but gets labelled anyway. You, however, find him fascinating, listening to his thoughts about life, and you spend many hours with him just walking and talking. At first, your parents think your friendship is quite harmless, but soon they become quite concerned when they hear whispers of marriage. Not only is he sickly, but he is only the third son. If you have married and he dies, you will be left with nothing. Your parents begin to pressure his family to keep him away from you, by whatever means necessary.*

"Despite your fear of your parents, you begin to meet this young man in secrecy. This is not easy when you both have servants, spinster aunts, and nosy friends who are more than willing to report on you. However, you do have an older brother who adores you and helps you get away from your home, enabling you to meet with your love. Your brother's name is either Robert or John. (Later on microfiche, I found John James, Katherine's older brother, christened May 21, 1665 in Petworth, Father, Robert; nine months older than Katherine.)

"It is impossible to meet in the village, so you begin meeting on the outskirts and, alone, you travel by cart into the country. He often has packages of food prepared by his cook. Your picnics together become very special. Opposition from your parents grows greater. I see the young man's grandfather here, forced to send his grandson away.

Since the young man is already thought of as ill, an excuse is readily made. He is allowed to see you once more to say good-bye and to explain to you the necessity of his going to a rest home. His health has not been good, so this is perfectly under-standable. What he does not know is that arrangements have been made for his placement in an asylum.

"A few weeks go by. You are called to the sitting room in your family's home. I see an enormous, elegant room with a white stone fire-place, heavy blue drapes, and white and blue panels on the walls. On one wall are long windows that overlook a terraced garden. Here you are given the news of his death. You cry, you scream, you are wild with fury. Your behaviour is totally inexcusable, and after a few days, no longer tolerated. In your parents' view, you are a silly nuisance. You are sent to live with an aunt. I see this aunt quite clearly. She is a tall, thin, cold woman, dressed in black, a white cap on her head. You call her Aunt Agatha. She is unmoved by your grief, and has only one so-lution, to give you laudanum, an opium solution, given for all pain, whether it be physical or mental. You are soon addicted and, although your aunt is ignorant of the signs—sweating and coughing—she still looks after you. She thinks she has succeeded where your parents have failed. You are no longer raving, but are quite tranquil. Your small body, not able to endure a prolonged drugged state, becomes increas-ingly frail. You die peacefully one afternoon, many weeks after hear-ing of the death of your young man. I should tell you that if he had not died, you would have done whatever was necessary to be together. You would have run away to another part of England."

I sat, quite stunned, as if emerging from a dream. The de-tailed scene Pet had described seemed so vivid and real, yet all I could manage to say was, "The room where I was told of his death was blue . . . the color blue has always made me so very sad . . ."

Pet leaned toward me, and quietly asked if she could guess who the young man from the 1600s was. She could see him clearly—before he was killed in his last life, and that right now he was part of the room, part of Petworth, he was completely surrounding us. "*He is John Lennon.*"

There was total silence in the room. I doubt whether any of us even breathed.

"You see, the reason for you living in this particular life is to live through the grief of John's death. You were unable to get over that grief before it was suppressed by the drug, and then dying yourself. Now in this lifetime, once you have expressed that grief, you must let it go. That will be the final step, letting it go. That was the last life time in which you were together physically. Spiritually, though, you have always been together and that's what really counts, isn't it?"

Pet paused, looking at me and then at Ros and Ann, as if deciding whether she should continue. "If Lennon had lived, if he had not been shot, he would have begun to talk of this somehow. I get the feeling he has confided in a friend or a member of his family, who knows why John's past had haunted him in his present."

I instantly became alert. "I do have a question. A story like this is hard to check out. Some stuff I have, like Katherine's birth record, but I'm not completely sure of John's name, only because I can't find a record of him in Petworth. I've found a record of a John Baron in Fittleworth, who may be his grandfather. Anyway, my question is, was his name John Baron?"

"His name was either John Baron or John Fitzherbert; now, sometimes, I'm completely wrong with names so you'll have to look into that yourself."

'Great,' I thought, 'I'm becoming convinced of John Lennon but I'm not so sure of the name John Baron.' I mulled over the name Fitzherbert. I'd never heard of it, but I'd add it to my list.

After thanking her and offering to pay her, she insisted, "No, I don't want money. Your search is genuine, and I'm happy to have helped. When people ask me to tell them if they'll get rich or stuff like that, then I take their money."

Pet drove off into the night. Ros, Ann, and I walked silently through the dark, winding lanes of Petworth. There was no traffic, the shops were closed, and the only sound came from the tapping of our shoes on the cobblestone street.

Finally, Ros broke the silence, asking if I was okay. I said I was overwhelmed. Only a short time before, I was dubious about John Baron being the same soul as John Lennon. Now, I was becoming sure. All I had to figure out now was if he was a Baron or a Fitzherbert!

Ann cut in, "Jewelle, I wanted to tell you this earlier, but I couldn't because Pet was there, and I thought it might interfere with her reading. This afternoon, after I left you and Ros at Peter Jerrome's, I went home and something quite strange happened. My daughter, Becky, came to me in the garden. You know, the daughter with the gift that I told you about this afternoon. I told her that a woman had come from Canada, and was looking for information on a past life. I just said, 'There's a woman here from Canada, who thinks she lived another life, here in Petworth. A few years ago, a man was killed' . . . and then Becky interrupted me, saying, *'shot* and *John Lennon.'* "

I was stunned. "Becky had seen John Lennon that quickly? You hadn't discussed it with her at all?"

Yes, Ann assured me, Becky had seen it all that quickly, and she would have had no way of knowing anything about me and my reason for being in Petworth. Ann was finding it all incredible; first Pet seeing John Lennon connected to me and then Becky seeing it too. At my request to meet with Becky, Ann said she didn't know if she would. "She's very shy about her gift, but I'll ask."

Reaching my lodgings I had the same sense of foreboding as

before, and was tempted to run after Ros and Ann. However, I made my way to my gloomy little room and collapsed on my bed.

A piercing scream woke me. As I sat up, the only sound in my room was the pounding of my heart. In the moonlight, I saw myself reflected in the mirror—pale skin, dark eyes and, for a moment, long hair. I put my hand to my head, fingering the short locks, and felt a shiver run the length of my spine. Of course, my hair wasn't long. I must have seen a shadow.

(Since Just Imagine *was published, many different individuals have come forward to share with me their similar feelings while lodging at the B & B; all had the same sense of foreboding when entering the attic room where Katherine had died.)*

Illegible headstones at St. Mary's Church (PHOTO: JOANNE ALARIC)

Eighteen

A lthough the arrival of morning brought me some relief, a cold chill continued to pervade my body as I sat alone over an early breakfast in the warm, sun-filled dining room. Barely noticing the home-made marmalade and whole wheat croissants, I was deep in thought when my hostess startled me by handing me a note.

Ros, on her way to work, had left a message saying that Ann's daughter, Becky, had agreed to meet me. I would find her on the corner of Market Square at 10:00. I was to look for a younger version of Ann. Ros' note also told me she had managed a meeting with Jumbo Taylor, a man very knowledgeable in Petworth's history. I was to meet him that evening at his residence, #5 Apple Lane.

The beautiful, young woman waiting for me in Market Square looked like she belonged in *Vogue Magazine*, not a small English village. Her blonde hair glowed like a halo in the bright sunshine. Somewhat reticently, she greeted me, stating she hoped she could be of some help. Her mother had given her scant details—a past life in Petworth, and my connection with John Lennon, which she had already seen.

Suggesting we begin by walking, Becky led the way through the busy lanes. The brilliant sunshine warmed us as we progressed, without talking, to the opposite side of the village. She slowed her pace, and stated she had a feeling we should go in the direction which she pointed out. I recognized the same alley I had walked with Ann and Ros, the one leading to Round the Hills. After a few minutes of walking along the path, overlooking the green valley, we approached a bench. Becky said, "My knees seem weak. I'm getting something. Let's sit here for a while. *I see a young girl with long dark hair ... "*

Looking straight ahead, but not seeing the valley before us, Becky started speaking in a voice no louder than a whisper. *"I feel excitement. You are waiting for someone to arrive from down there."* She pointed to the traces of the old road to Fittleworth. *"You are waiting for a man who comes to Petworth along this road. I see you waving. He sees you and waves back. There is a bond, a united love between you."*

Becky stood up quickly and suggested we keep walking. I didn't say a word, afraid to break her concentration. As we walked further along the path, I noticed her sad expression and tears swelling up in her eyes. *"I can feel your loneliness. You are walking by yourself. He has given you bad news. He has to go away. You probably won't see him again. You're in deep despair. You keep looking back toward the valley, hoping to see him once more, but he's already gone."*

The path suddenly turned back onto a lane, but instead of taking the route back to the village centre, Becky felt we should follow a road away from town. Once again, we walked parallel to the beautiful valley. We came across a plain house that caught our attention. The gray house sat at the edge of a field overlooking the valley beyond. We couldn't see the end of the house, but I instantly knew it had a window at its furthest end. Becky was frightened. She didn't want to continue, but I had to see the window. Becky reluctantly agreed, saying that psychically, she, too, could see a window. She said it had been my room, and I had spent hours just looking across the valley. Suddenly, time seemed to stop, our movements were like a dream, everything was in slow motion.

Finally, we reached the front of the ordinary house. The window was gone! It had been plastered over, but its outline was still very visible. I told Becky we had to find out about the house.

An elderly woman, wearing Wellingtons and an old house dress, approached us from nowhere. "Excuse me," I asked, trying to use my most polite tone, "could you tell us about that gray house? I noticed that the front window has been removed and plastered over. I wonder why anybody would cover such a beautiful view? And could you tell us what year this house was built?"

"You young ladies needn't be poking around here asking questions. That house is from the 1800s, and that's all I'm about to tell you." She put her hands on her hips, ending our conversation.

Becky and I hurried back to the road, and began our journey back to the town centre. Only when we were out of the woman's earshot did we burst into nervous laughter. I wondered what that was all about. The whole scene had seemed like a bad dream.

I knew that house was definitely connected to me, but the 1800s? I was beginning to see that Petworth possibly has many hidden secrets for me, some that could take a lifetime to uncover. That house was one of them.

We were heading in the direction of St. Mary's Church and as we walked, my mind kept coming back to my suspicions about possibly having lived more than one life in southern England. I didn't question Becky about this, but I kept wondering: how many lives had I lived? Not only in southern England, but in Petworth?

As we approached St. Mary's Church, Becky motioned for me to follow her through the churchyard. We sat in the shade of a giant oak tree. Becky spoke again, saying that many conversations between the young man and me took place here. He had many ideas to share, ideas that many people of the day thought were mad, but I listened to him and took him seriously. Becky's words began to blur. It seemed that everyone who was psychically involved in seeing my past life, all had pretty much the same story. Sure, there were a few different aspects, but the basic story was the same, whether it was seen by Becky or Pet, Konni or Mom. A young couple madly in love, small village in England hundreds of years ago, parted tragically by the young man's death. The pain of parting was so great that their love was unable to die.

Leaving the churchyard, we walked along Petworth's most ancient and only cobblestoned lane, Lombard Street, toward Market Square. I took the opportunity to ask Becky whether she was familiar with the song, *Jealous Guy*. She was not, and I explained that when I first heard it, I had a vivid mental picture of lush green grass surrounding a milestone. In response, she told me that Petworth had had a milestone, but it had been hit by a lorry some years ago. Now a plaque had been erected in its place. She offered to show me. This was unexpected! I hadn't thought of checking out the milestone. What else had I forgotten? The chimes! But Becky knew nothing about chimes. I snapped a photo of the plaque which bore the simple phrase, *49 miles to London.*

Becky and I walked through Market Square to Golden Square. With a puzzled look on her face, she sniffed the air. "I can smell fresh bread, but there's no smell in the air is there?" No, there wasn't, but I recalled that during my regression, the first scene was of me standing in that very square carrying a basket of bread! Becky's response to this was a fleeting smile.

Golden Square has a book store, and I smiled when I noticed their address, *The Old Bakery*.

It occurred to me to ask Becky about one more location, and we were once again on the move. We stopped across the lane from my bed and breakfast, and I explained that the place had been giving me the creeps! Suggesting we walk around the exterior of the building, she declined my invitation to go inside, stating that something very bad had happened there. I tried to joke about the fact that I had one more night to spend there, but there was no smile from Becky as she insisted she didn't feel good about the place.

Approaching the back of the house, she pointed up to a small, gabled window and said, "Right there! Something is wrong!" Unable to suppress my surprise, I told her the gabled window was where the staircase turned and led to my room, and how whenever I went up those stairs I dreaded it, and every day the feeling was getting stronger.

"Is that your room at the top? It was then, too. You were a prisoner in that room, kept there against your will. I see an elderly woman, an aunt. My God!" Becky shuddered. "You *died* in that room!"

I stared up at the building, knowing fate had brought me back to where it had all ended for Katherine James—her love, her dreams, her life. With a sick feeling in my stomach, I wondered how I would survive another night in the cold attic room.

After Becky departed, I slowly wandered back to Golden Square. I found a little delicatessen and purchased ginger beer and meat pies. I returned to the bench where Becky and I had sat, overlooking Round the Hills. I ate lunch, indulging in fantasy. I sat alone where Katherine had sat, waiting for her love. The valley glimmered in the afternoon sun as I gazed at the ancient road to Fittleworth. My eyes swelled with tears, knowing that today no one would be traveling down the road towards me.

Wearily, I left the beautiful valley, walking the long route back through the village.

I had been avoiding North Street, a winding street with ancient buildings on one side which hid the view of the sloping valley and faced onto the dark stone wall of the Petworth House grounds on the other. It was time I took a walk around the area. As I walked beside the renovated Thompson's Hospital I had no feeling at all. However, on the same street, a tall, narrow red brick building caught my attention. A sign said, *Sommerset Hospital.*

The traffic was annoying, and I felt suffocated as I was compelled to walk several times back and forth in front of the brick building. To me, it felt ghoulish and evil. A small porch enclosed two wooden benches and beyond, a dark, heavy oak door. I recognized the door. I knocked but there was no answer. I was angry, angrier than I'd ever felt. I wanted to scream, "Open the door! I know you're in there!" Was I angry at past ghosts or angry at my past memories that seemed to refuse to come out?

I have yet to solve the mystery of the hospitals. Just before leaving Petworth, I went to the library and read an article titled, Some Buildings of Petworth. . . . Sommerset Hospital, dating from the 16th Century, has its "Original Door" from 1654. I knew it! Part of me wished that Becky and I had gone to the street with the hospitals, but part of me wanted to leave well enough alone. I had been correct about the door, a door that Katherine would have seen, and again I knew there were parts of Petworth unexplainable to me. Yes, Jewelle, leave well enough alone. The rattling of too many ghosts could prove detrimental to your mental health!

A mauve and purple dusk fell on Petworth as I knocked on the door of #5 Apple Lane. I introduced myself to the blue eyed husky man who answered the door. He invited me into the warm kitchen, and had me sit at a small oval table near the crackling stove. I explained my interest in Petworth history was confined to the period of the late 1600s. Jumbo Taylor's warm and encouraging manner made me go to the heart of the matter. I ended with telling him that checking out the history of Petworth was a way of confirming my past life in Petworth. I asked him if this quest of mine surprised him. "No, I'm sure we all have many lifetimes. Your story is no surprise at all."

Greatly relieved, I asked him if I could start asking questions. Did he know of the James family during the 1600s? He confirmed they were a well established family in Petworth during that period. Did he know anything of the early history of my bed and breakfast, the Grange House? Part of the house had been added in the late 1700s, but the original part pre-dated 1600. At one time it may have been servants' quarters for domestic help working at Petworth House.

I told him of my confusion with Petworth House. Although I had no familiar feelings towards the massive stone house, itself, I did feel connected to the many black wrought iron plaques that lined the low corridor walls within the House.

Mr. Taylor explained that the plaques were a collection of inserts from fireplaces used in the 1600s, Katherine's time.

I was puzzled. "Why wouldn't the House be a memory; it's so gigantic, so imposing?"

"When did Katherine James die?"

"1683."

He smiled. "Petworth House was rebuilt in 1688. You wouldn't have memories of the present House. It was rebuilt after you died!"

I felt in a mild state of shock as I continued to ask questions. I asked Jumbo if he might be able to identify a route or roadway if I read a description from *Katherine's Story*. After I read the passage, he indicated it was possible, and went to fetch a map. Spreading out a large scale map of Petworth and the surrounding area, he showed me the Road to Chichester. At my question, he said that was how the road was known. He showed me how one would follow that road and turn off at a field, and that the cliffs I mentioned were probably the abandoned quarry, now grown over. All that I had written was possible!

I read another passage. Jumbo looked in a drawer and another map emerged, one of Petworth in the 1600s. He pointed out the hospital. Then he proceeded to show where the ancient stone bridge had been. It had been rebuilt, but its original foundations were still there. The wild flowers, he stated, were probably foxglove, an old variety native to the area, which grow all over in the summer.

My head was spinning. Foxglove! Patrick White! Was he part of this? My dream of Patrick flashed before me, requesting foxglove be put on his grave . . . and of my reading with Cecilia so many years ago, when Patrick had said that in time I would understand. I would have to digest all this later. There was still more to hear from Jumbo.

Were there any chimes in Petworth in the 1600s? Market Square had had a water clock. Time was marked in intervals by the ringing of chimes. These chimes could be heard all over the village. My mother's words of chimes echoed in my mind. Her words faded as Konni's voice came to mind with her story of chimes.

I was doing my best to keep my emotions in check as question after question was being answered. "Were there any asylums in the Petworth area at that time?"

Mr. Taylor's response to this was one word, "Plenty." He elaborated that, in those days, an asylum was simply a place to remove a person from society, for mental or physical reasons. "Asylum" did not necessarily mean a mental institution, but merely a place of confinement. *I later learned there were actual "asylum carts" that transported patients to these institutions. I*

remembered that my mother had mentioned John being taken away
in a cart, and Pet had said he was taken to an asylum. I could only
imagine where John may have died and felt, hundreds of years later,
sick at the thought of his pain.

When I took leave of the soft-spoken Englishman, I thanked
him effusively for his time and his information. He had verified
so much more than I had ever hoped for. He assured me that
the pleasure was his because he enjoyed every opportunity to
talk about the history of his town.

All was quiet at Grange House when I let myself in and crept
up the stairs. The cold chill grew stronger with each step. I
could feel the old woman's presence. I sat down on the top step
to deal with Aunt Agatha.

I hissed into the night, "Go away, Auntie! Did you think you
and Rachel could hide this forever? I'm in control now! You
can go to hell!" The cold chill which had hovered about me
since my arrival, seemed to disappear. Whether or not it was a
case of mind over matter, I was able to go to bed in relative
peace.

The moon shone through the narrow window, embracing
my attic room in a soft, silver glow. So very long ago, had Katherine laid in this very room, as John Baron watched over her,
waiting for her to die? Tonight was he also watching and waiting, this time not for Katherine's death, but for her to begin to
live?

I awoke to my last day in Petworth, watching the first traces
of the morning light blanketing the little town. Triumphantly,
I looked around the room. It was just a room, no longer a sinis-
ter prison guarded by a strong willed and misguided aunt.

Another note from Ros invited me over for Sunday lunch at
1:00. I was happy to spend my last day in Petworth with this
special woman. She wanted to know how things had gone with
Becky. I was still amazed at how my day had gone with both

Becky and Jumbo Taylor as I shared with Ros my discoveries, detail by detail. Having talked to Jumbo, she already knew of the Road to Chichester and the cliffs. She offered to show them to me after lunch.

"Lunch" was roast beef and Yorkshire pudding, followed by trifle for dessert. "Ros, that was the best lunch I've ever had. At home, lunch is a sandwich and . . . oh, I'm going to miss you." I began to cry.

"Now, now, enough of that," she fussed, handing me a tissue. "Let's go on that walk."

For the first time since my arrival, the sunshine had given way to a light rain. As Ros and I walked through a field leading to a trail, she pointed to where the foxglove grew each summer. All I could do was visualize a riot of color in the field. Then I sensed something familiar and slowed. Here were the trees along the river, and as we rounded the curve in the path, the bridge. Shrieking, I ran to the middle of the bridge, looking back towards Ros who was pointing out the ancient stone foundations, the only remaining part of the original bridge. Enormous oak trees gave way to a thin pine forest, as Ros commented, "In the spring, this is known as the Bluebell Wood."

Bluebells! I'd forgotten Konni's last words as I left for England. "You loved bluebells." As with the foxglove I had missed the season, but again had found a piece of Katherine's past. The land suddenly seemed to have become a giant bowl. We were standing in the middle of the ancient quarry, now grown over in soft green. We began to climb up the steep grade, laughing as we slipped and climbed over dead trees, finally reaching the high ground. I turned around and gasped. The earth looked as if it had fallen away before us. It was all so familiar. I could see the whole countryside, another small village in the distance, the Bluebell Wood, and the expanse of soft, rolling hills miles away. I saw beside us a farmer's field with the Road to Chichester in the distance. I was in Ros' arms, sobbing uncontrollably with a painful kind of joy. "I'm home, Ros, I'm home, and if I never see this beautiful place again, I'll always know where home is!"

"Jewelle, remember that home is where the heart is." Through the years that followed, when I returned to Petworth again and again, did I truly know, this was my home.

As fog would dissipate on a sunny day, a veil seemed to lift. I could see Ros clearly, as clearly as I had seen Robert Philp, the same soul as Peter Jerrome.

I thought of Ros' concern, her loving kindness as she arranged contact with all the people who could help me rediscover my past. This person had also cared for me once, long, long ago. I could only smile with delight as my eyes rested on the loving face of my dear Polly, Katherine's nanny.

Somehow, I said my farewells to Ros and to Petworth. My search was over.

I boarded the silver jet for my journey back to Canada. My eyes were heavy, as my mind sped through the events of the past week.

A passenger, directly in front of me, annoyingly crumpled his newspaper and held it up so high that the headlines stared at me. *Patrick White Dies.* Stunned, I stared back. An Australian novelist. What did I expect? *My* Patrick White?

I replayed my week in Petworth. "Damn," I muttered, remembering Pet telling me she wasn't very good with names. Groaning inwardly, I did not relish investigating John's surname.

Arriving in Vancouver, I spent the night at my mother's. As I retrieved a souvenir for her from my bag, she also had something for me. A sweatshirt. "Thanks," I said politely, examining the white shirt with painted ski bunnies on it. Then something caught my eye. In tiny letters, written under the bunnies, was a copyright symbol and the words, "*John Baron!*"

My Baron or Fitzherbert question was answered. I later realized that in a matter of ten hours both names, Patrick White and John Baron, had been brought to my attention. A mystery that I would later have to ponder.

Despite raw emotions and jet lag, I reached for pen and paper. A single tear slid down my cheek as I began to write, "So you think you've lived a past life with John Lennon?"

Nineteen

Months passed. I was consumed by an incredible drive to record my experiences of the past decade, as time became a blur of words on paper. I wondered what drove me on and, years later, this still eludes me. Finally, when all had been written and recorded, I titled the manuscript, *Just Imagine*. Placing the box of typed papers in the back of my closet to begin collecting dust, I wept as if I had lost a dear friend.

Through the time of writing I had become friends with Sara and Dihane. Sara owned the local bookstore; Dihane was my next door neighbor.

A year after returning from Petworth, Sara introduced me to Judy, a psychic and channeler. Sara had arranged for Judy to give me a reading, after closing time, in the back of the tiny bookstore. It was in the dead of winter, and as I entered the shop the only light came from a snow-covered street lamp which cast a blue hue on the shelves of books. The night already seemed magical!

Judy immediately put me at ease as she explained her ability to receive messages from both her guides and departed ones through automatic writing. Judy's first observation was that I was writing a book and she declared there would be many books. I thought that surviving the completion of one book would be a miracle, but kept silent.

Judy asked me if I had any questions. I asked her to tell me about John Baron, a man I had loved in a past life. I mentioned how a British psychic had said that in his recent life, John had confided in someone close to him of his recollections of this same past life.

Judy responded, saying that John Baron was no longer in this world, but was in the spirit world; but who knew about his recollections of a past life? I watched, mesmerized, as Judy wrote in large, flowing letters, *Mother knows.*

The meaning of *Mother knows* took me about thirty seconds to understand. I gasped. John Lennon's pet name for Yoko Ono was *Mother.* I blurted, "Tell me about John Lennon!"

Judy looked mildly surprised as her pen began to flow. *I talk to Julian.* I swallowed hard as the writing continued. *Julian talks to me. He will laugh at you (Jewelle), but tell him to check with Lucy. Yoko has seen me, she has seen my spirit and will know this is a true message. Yoko will wonder what you want from her.*

"Well," I said, "she probably thinks that about a lot of people, but it's not like I'll be discussing it with her or anything."

"Yes, you will," Judy said, "you will be meeting Yoko. I can see it in your aura."

Judy continued, "John says he talks to you, Jewelle. Is that true?"

My head felt light. "Yes, indirectly, through my sister," I said. The little room seemed to fill with light and an enveloping love. For the first time since discovering Petworth, I felt the presence of my long-lost John Baron.

Judy leaned towards me, "I can see John beside you, his arm is around your shoulder. Remember, your story is never ending."

Days later the short, yet intense, experience was still on my mind. I wrote a note to Judy, thanking her for the reading. Not only did I receive a reply from Judy, but a message from John Baron as well.

I had told Judy nothing of my past life story other than England being the location and John Baron being my lost love. Reading Judy's letter for the hundredth time, I was amazed at the common thread that had also wound its way through Konni's messages and even my own recollections.

Dear Jewelle,

Hi, thanks for your welcome letter. I have to say that I am really impressed with your project, and I do see the stress it has caused and will cause. Also, I see you gaining strength from your work.

I have messages for you from your soul mate. I feel like a bit of an intruder here, but I will quote word for word . . .

"John here, for my beloved Jewelle, arms open for you to receive. Long ago our souls were eternally connected for the development of our futures. Do not feel it necessary to see me as I was, nor should you always compare our lives to establish parallels. This seems a futile exercise. I ask that you listen for the present time and for the future of your existence on this earth plane, for now. Yes, I feel your frustration of the task you have chosen to get through to the people. Remember, I, too, tried in my own way to get messages out that I received and used as songs.

For this message, I will be happy to let you know that I will help you access your light within, for it is only with the faith of that which is unseen that you reach out to the faith of others. The energy must be compatible to create. Your nature is to love and trust, but more than once I have felt your tears of frustration with the world."

Jewelle (this is Judy), he says, "Dance with me, my beloved . . . John."

Your friend,
Judy

Dance? Dance was the single word that John Baron could have used, and did use, as a password, to reach me.

A week later, a letter arrived from Ann in Petworth. I expected a cheery letter filled with news and gossip; instead my hands began shaking as I read.

Dear Jewelle,

Ros and I are writing this letter together. We had decided to have a psychic circle evening with Pet and Becky. Pet, however, couldn't make it so Becky's friend, Sophie, came instead. Sophie wrote down words, from John, that came out of Becky's mouth. We have enclosed all the details. We only wish that you could have been here. It was all very personal, we felt like eavesdroppers.

Fondest Love,
Ann and Ros

I tried to calmly read the messages, while realizing that John had simultaneously channeled through two sources—one in British Columbia, one in England, both messages unsolicited by me.

"John here. It's me again, just a different channel. The dancing hasn't stopped. Still dancing with you, just a different place. Arms around your waist. With your hair smelling sweetly. Do you remember violet flowers? Smell of hair, curls in hair, ringlets and blue ribbon? Blue dress and choker around neck. Waltz music. Dark eyes."

Then,

"This is for you, Katherine."

"Through flowers and songs
I give her my heart
Katherine, my dear
So sweet and so mild

Oh, so tender my love
You are just a child."

John adds, "Katherine, come back to Petworth. Your roots are
there. We'll walk together along the road where we weren't allowed
to walk, hand in hand."

Slowly I tucked away the notes and letter from Ann.

Later, Konni said, "This is beyond coincidence." As usual, I
only gave partial credence to the fact that John Baron was
reaching out to me from the spirit world.

"Don't be afraid to totally accept this," Konni would say.

"You're right," I would mumble to Konni, "but besides, I
have real problems—my impending divorce."

Twenty

T he old tune *Breaking Up is Hard to Do* pretty well summed up the next year. Bob and I had completed our journey together, I would philosophize, as we began the painful dismantling of our marriage.

I moved to Salmon Arm, a nearby town on the Shuswap Lake, to begin a new life. My days were spent soul searching, taking long walks by the lake, and my nights were usually spent in tears. Reluctantly, I accepted that a state of grieving had to be endured before a new life could begin.

Konni called, asking me in a tone that only a sister can get away with. "What about your book? Are you going to wait until you're eighty to have it published?" Visualizing myself as a Miss Haversham, with a box of yellow typed papers, brittle with age, I laughed despite my state of gloom.

Konni's words played on my mind as I took a baby step in a new direction. I joined the *Shuswap Writers' Group*, a bunch of lively and intelligent women and men. Here I met Moira, whose deep blue eyes and platinum blonde hair were as striking as her personality. Moira, who had left her husband of thirty-five years, had also just moved to the Shuswap area to start anew. Moira, who in the psychic world is known as Victoria, taught me to trust in a loving Universe that provides for us all. This "trusting the Universe" was a new concept for me and I tried to practice her advice. Moira insisted that we are given signs and direction daily, if we only care to listen and pay attention.

I landed a job in Healthcare and wondered if this was my new direction.

Konni called again, practically shouting, "The book, Jewelle, get the damn book out."

Later, Moira laughed and said, "The Universe is trying, through Konni, to wake you up."

That night, I slowly carried my dusty manuscript from the closet floor to the kitchen table. Thumbing through the pages, I realized that through my marital breakdown, I had nearly forgotten about Katherine and John. Konni, however, had not.

June, 1995, fifteen years after John Lennon had been shot, my new book, *Just Imagine*, sat proudly on local bookstore shelves.

I should have felt at peace, and had a sense of accomplishment, but this wasn't the case. Now that my story was public, I felt no different than I had during my early days of searching. I was still afraid, and even embarrassed, to shout to the world, "Yes, I knew John Lennon in a past life, where he was John Baron and I was Katherine James."

Konni quipped, "Your manuscript came out of the closet, but you have not."

Yes, that was it. Oh sure, I went on radio, did newspaper interviews, had book signing parties, and even went on TV once where I thought I'd die before the five minutes was up. Despite my shyness, readers loved the book. Thank God for that!

Now, I didn't know which direction to take with *Just Imagine*, or if I even wanted to. A reprieve from planning any future came in an unexpected early morning overseas call from Ros, in

Petworth. The *Petworth Society* was inviting me over to England for a book signing party, to be held in November. I burst into happy tears.

In November, 1995, upon arriving in England a week preceding the party, all felt magical. So many members of the *Petworth Society* had made a special effort to welcome me and *Just Imagine*; from being stopped on the street with words of congratulations, to an anonymous poem written by a local lady, depicting the centuries' old lives of John and Katherine. The local newspaper sent a reporter around and an interview with BBC *Radio* had been arranged.

Throughout this week, coincidentally, the *Beatles Anthology* had been released and each night I watched John and the other Beatles on Ros' telly.

The night of the book signing party arrived. My British friends had sent an invitation to Paul McCartney, who lives in Sussex, to the party. Paul didn't come, of course, but we were having fun. God, it felt good to laugh again!

Entering the ancient town hall, I felt humbled. The ambiance was perfect. A circle of chairs faced an oval table, covered by an Irish lace cloth. Accompanying the table was a Queen Anne chair, where I would sit to read excerpts from *Just Imagine* to the audience. Behind burgundy velvet drapes, hiding a stage, John Lennon's *Imagine* played softly. Completing the scene was a grand piano adorned by a bouquet of flowers, John Lennon's photograph, and several copies of *Just Imagine*.

Peter Jerrome, the chairman of the *Petworth Society*, stood to make a speech; the same Peter whom I'd approached on my first trip to Petworth, five years earlier, inquiring about life in Petworth in the 1600s. I smiled, remembering. Peter must have thought me mad! Now, Peter was instrumental in organizing this evening, enabling me to bring my story home. As Peter began to speak, I gazed into the sea of faces—to Ros and her husband, John, to Ann and Becky, and my eyes filled with tears. I tried to absorb Peter's words.

"The first thing you have to say is that this is a very courageous effort, the second is that it is very much a Petworth book, one like no other, the third, it is extremely readable. Simply put, the basic premise of the book is preposterous.

John Lennon of the Beatles was shot dead in New York City just before 11 o'clock on December 8, 1980. Jewelle Lewis, a Canadian housewife, several years Lennon's junior, had no more than a passing interest in the group, other than planning to see them in Vancouver in 1964 and being disappointed when the trip failed to materialize. She was, therefore, disconcerted to find her grief at Lennon's sudden death was boundless and uncontrollable, and lasted through the 80s. Jewelle had known John Lennon in a previous life and a first trip to England in 1985 was to Mere in Wiltshire. It proved largely abortive. Jewelle, however, refused to abandon her quest to make sense of the turmoil she was in and further psychic enquiry suggested not only that the century, but also the location, had been incorrect on her initial trip. The century was the 17th, rather than the 15th, and the location West Sussex. John Lennon had been one John Baron, and Jewelle had been Katherine James. They had been engaged to be married, but John died of consumption. Katherine had tended him for a time before dying herself of grief (and) heavily dosed on laudanum by an aunt. Jewelle returned to England in 1990, armed with more information about the James family and allied matters. As chairman of the Society, I had already corresponded with her, but remained somewhat uneasy about her central thesis. Ros Staker was a tower of strength for Jewelle, as was Ann Boxall and her daughter, Becky. Ros brought Jewelle around to see me and Jewelle writes, "Although he had the reserved, polite manner characteristic of English men, I sensed a doubtfulness in his expression as Ros introduced us." Couldn't have said it better myself. A visit to Jumbo Taylor added some detail, but I'm not going to spoil the book by telling you more. It reads like a detective story and it has real Petworth people in it, as well as their 17th Century counterparts. Perhaps it tells us as much about Petworth in the 1990s, as about Petworth in the 1600s. That's for you to judge. I remain uneasy about the basic thesis, but it's a real talking-point. I enjoyed reading it and its certainly not as silly as it sounds. Jewelle's had the courage to write it and get it published, and the book itself is its own tribute to her drive and perseverance. However cynical you may be, it does raise interesting questions and it makes you think. How many books do that? Read it, you'll enjoy it."

The flight from London to Vancouver was a pleasant one. I watched the flight attendant slowly push a silver cart, as my mind played over the events of the past week. The book signing party in Petworth had been the happiest night of my life. The people of Petworth had honored John and Katherine, for which I am eternally grateful.

As British Columbia's rugged terrain came into view, I felt my search was over. Or so I thought.

Twenty-one

As the plane gently descended into Vancouver, I viewed the scenery through the eyes of passengers arriving in western Canada for the first time. The Pacific Ocean rippled in silver and Vancouver Island in the distance, greeted the many Europeans eager to view the wilds of British Columbia. For me, these flights between London and Vancouver were journeys across the centuries. Katherine in Sussex was Jewelle in B.C., and with each trip the transition became easier.

Before leaving the airport, I stopped at a bank machine. The numbers on the ATM screen only reinforced the old adage, "don't quit your day job," which is exactly what I had done in those rose-colored days when I visualized myself promoting and supporting myself with a paperback.

Hailing a taxi, too tired to care about money, I arrived at my mother's an hour later where I immediately fell into bed.

The next morning, over coffee, I shared with my mom all the excitement of my book party. I also began confiding in her that I was broke and had no job, when the phone rang interrupting our conversation. The call was for me, and later as I hung up my mom asked with concern, "Anything wrong?"

"Wrong?" I said, dumbfounded, "no, in fact, everything is right. A friend, Maureen, has offered me a job."

"What kind of job?"

"Living with, and caring for, Maureen's husband's aunt. Audrey, is her aunt's name; she has terminal cancer and her wish is to die at home. Maureen says the job could last a month or a year."

"And you were just saying you had no job . . ." my mother trailed off, for I had already left the room to gather my luggage together.

That afternoon I left the West Coast and travelled inland, by Greyhound, to Eagle Bay, a small community on the Shuswap Lake close to Salmon Arm. As the bus inched up the steep mountain grade of the Coquihalla highway, I could hear Moira's voice, "Trust in the Universe to provide." Looking out of the bus window, I raised my eyes to the deep blue sky and whispered, "Thank you."

That night Maureen introduced me to Audrey, a refined, quiet woman in her early seventies. Over the next few days I settled into Audrey's world and into my room in her country home.

To me, Audrey didn't seem like a dying woman, except for her small appetite and frequent naps. Our morning routine began with Audrey's breakfast, served on a linen-covered tray, which I carried to her room. Throughout the day, I administered to her needs, supplied her room with fresh towels and clean sheets, and spent time beside her bed where we chatted like old friends. My new life, caring for Audrey in her home seemed so comfortable and familiar. So very familiar.

Audrey's family visited daily, took care of shopping, doctors' appointments, and all outside chores, but for the most of the day it was just Audrey and me. As time went by, Audrey slept more and more, and I spent many hours alone.

Spring had arrived. One lazy afternoon I spent endless minutes watching a hummingbird dart back and forth to a bright red feeder which adorned Audrey's sun deck. I realized, that for months, I had not slowed down enough to simply *be* and enjoy life's small pleasures.

Through these days I began to indulge myself in another long forgotten pleasure—reading the works of my favorite authors, the Brontës.

The country nights were conducive to pondering and reminiscing. I often sat on the sun deck, wrapped in a blanket and curled up on a lounge chair, with a baby monitor nearby to alert me to any change in Audrey's breathing from her nearby bedroom.

One such evening I stared into the dark, while a choir of unseen frogs serenaded me and one of Audrey's horses whinnied softly. My thoughts flickered from one thing to another.

I visualized the Brontës, who lived a hundred years or more ago on the wild moors of northern England in Yorkshire. These motherless children, daughters and a son of Reverend Patrick Brontë, spent their secluded lives writing, drawing, storytelling, roaming the moors, and enjoying each other's company. Emily Brontë, who wrote *Wuthering Heights*, was my favorite.

My train of thought went to Herma, a lady whom I had met while belonging to a genealogy group. Herma had been doing her family genealogy, researching her roots, while I was searching for the existence of John and Katherine. Our common interest, however, was not genealogy, but psychic abilities. I asked Herma if she would like to test hers.

"Sure, that will be fun," she replied.

"Can you tell me who I was in a past life?" I asked.

"I'll try," Herma giggled. "I'll call you later."

The night was becoming cooler and I wrapped the blanket more tightly around myself. Audrey's breathing remained steady through the monitor.

Herma called me an hour later. Although the conversation took place many years ago, my memory of it has remained vivid. "Did you get a past life name for me?" I asked, expecting Katherine.

"No," Herma said slowly, "not a name, only initials."

Anticipating *K* or *C*, Herma announced, *E*. Before I could question her further, she added, "Actually, it's *E.B.*"

"*E.B.?*" I repeated, hiding my disappointment.

"Yes," Herma's voice was confident, "*E.B.* is connected to you in some way."

Herma must have ESP, I decided, for just that day I had been reading a biography of Emily Brontë. *E.B.* I decided to test Herma further. The next night I drove to Herma's with the Emily Brontë biography tucked in my bag. I had used masking tape to cover all identifying words on the book cover, leaving only Emily's portrait visible. I didn't know at the time, driving to Herma's, that this would be a night to remember.

Herma's home, tucked amongst the trees at the end of a long driveway, was a calm refuge from a busy world. We sat on over-stuffed couches, sipping chamomile tea.

"Herma, I want to show you something, " I began, reaching into my bag for Emily's biography. "I'm going to show you a portrait of a lady—just tell me whatever comes to mind, okay?" Herma nodded. I held up the book, covered in masking tape, revealing only Emily Brontë's image.

Five seconds passed before Herma blurted, "John Lennon was her brother."

"What?" I exclaimed.

Herma continued, "In another life of John Lennon's, he had been this lady's brother."

I called Konni the next day.

"Are you going to check it out?" Konni asked.

"What's to check out? Herma and I were just fooling

around. It all started when I asked her if she'd like to test her psychic abilities."

"Tell me this," Konni said, "did Emily Brontë have a brother?"

"Yes, his name was Branwell."

"Don't you think it's odd that John's name popped up, even when you were just fooling around?"

"I guess so," I mumbled.

"Do me a favor, okay? Just for fun. Go and see what similarities, if any, there are between John Lennon and Branwell Brontë."

It would be easier to research Branwell than argue with my sister, I decided, promising to report back. I called Konni a week later.

I began by admitting I had been surprised by Herma's revelations, but that I hadn't taken any of them seriously . . . until the self portraits, that is.

"What self portraits?" Konni questioned.

"I did as you suggested and began to research Branwell."

"And . . . ?" Konni asked.

"Branwell, like John, was an artist and a poet. Branwell drank and did drugs, actually he did more than doing drugs, he was an addict. Branwell, like John, lost his mother at a young age, and had sisters but no brothers. Oh, and Branwell had good friends in Liverpool. Branwell drew self portraits, what are they called?"

"Caricatures?" Konni offered.

"Yes, Branwell and John both drew caricatures, depicting aspects of their lives."

"Okay," said Konni, "it does sound like John Lennon in all ways, but it could be a thousand other guys, too. So, what's the clincher? I know you've got one."

"The clincher, my dear know-it-all sister, is this. Branwell's self portraits are the image of John Lennon. The nose, the glasses, everything!"

Although Konni was in far away California, I could practically see her smug smile as she said, "I *told* you that checking out the similarities between John and Branwell might prove interesting!"

I jumped at the crackling noise through the baby monitor as Audrey began coughing. The John/Branwell incident was already years old and would probably remain a mystery, I decided.

Audrey's family knew that time was running out for their dear aunt and never once did they falter in their dedication to fulfil her last wish—to die peacefully at home. Audrey's last weeks were filled with comforts that could never be provided in a hospital; her cat curled at her feet, the nearby whiny of her horse, and watching her favorite soap, *The Young and the Restless*, in the comfort of her own bed. Various members of Audrey's family dropped in each day, but Marie was the niece I saw regularly. Marie lived close by and, since my arrival, she had checked in daily on Audrey and me.

One day I sensed Marie staring at me. "What?" I laughed nervously.

"Oh," she smiled, "I can just see you doing home care hundreds of years ago, bustling about in a long black skirt with your hair in a bun."

Looking down at my slacks and t-shirt, I was at a loss for words. Marie and I had become close friends, so I took her observation in stride and thought no more of her comment.

Audrey was deteriorating rapidly and was now on morphine. She began reporting sightings from the "other side," and spoke of receiving comforting words from her departed mother. One morning Audrey told Marie of a dream, so real and vivid that it stayed with her. "It was so clear. A little girl came to me, asking me to take her hand. The girl wanted me to follow her down a flowered garden path. I told the girl I wasn't ready to come with her, not yet anyway. Isn't that the oddest dream?" Audrey concluded, with a wistful faraway smile. Later, Marie, Maureen, and I agreed—Audrey's time was drawing near.

A letter arrived from Konni, written by a friend. My sister seemed so far away, and it was comforting to read the friendly letter. Konni's friend had enclosed an ad of an American psychic, who claimed to have channeled the spirit of John Lennon. Staring at a photo of an attractive blonde woman in her forties, I wondered what she would think of my past life story with John. I tucked the article away in a flight bag that was stored with my luggage in Audrey's basement.

A nightmare awoke me. My heart pounded and I was disoriented until I realized the raspy, groaning sound was real and was coming from the baby monitor. I stumbled to Audrey's bedside. The oxygen tubing had fallen and precious air was not reaching the dying woman's lungs. With shaking hands I replaced the tubing, and Audrey's moans were soon replaced by quieter breathing.

The clock said three a.m., but I couldn't return to my bed. I was totally freaked out. I wanted to run away; I'd had enough. Death was all around me. The Audrey I had earlier met and had grown fond of, had now been replaced by a shell of her former self. I had made an employment commitment, but now I felt trapped. Only when the sun came up did I begin to feel better.

I spent no more nights on the sun deck. The TV was my constant companion; silly sitcoms, anything with laughter. Then, thankfully, Audrey's niece began to spend the nights with me. We shared the night duties, and I was so grateful not to be alone.

One morning, as the sun shone through the bedroom window casting a golden glow over Audrey's face, the dying woman's soul peacefully slipped away. Marie immediately felt her aunt's presence being replaced by a beautiful scent of roses.

Throughout the day as Audrey's family gathered, I went quietly to my room and began packing my belongings. Through my tears I knew I'd lived this scenario many times in different locations.

Audrey's funeral was on a warm, sunny June afternoon in 1996. The country church was filled as the community of Eagle Bay came to say goodbye to Audrey Sloan, a dignified, gentle country woman.

My job was over and it was time to leave. For months I had remained strong while Audrey slipped away. After all, it had been my job. What I hadn't realized was the toll it had taken on my emotions—witnessing the slow departure of another human being. I also felt blessed to have seen the love of a family, Audrey's family, and to have really understood how love can provide whatever is necessary; in this case, to have fulfilled Audrey's final wish.

Now, I had to take care of myself. I knew of only one way and one place in which to nurture my soul. I booked a flight to England. As I drove along the shoreline of the lake, away from Eagle Bay, I flipped on the car radio. There was John singing *All You Need Is Love*.

Twenty-two

Leaving Eagle Bay, I turned left onto the Trans-Canada Highway toward Revelstoke. The next three weeks I would spend with Joanne before flying to England. Being in Revelstoke is not a hardship in June, and I eagerly anticipated seeing friends and family again.

Joanne, now with her own family, welcomed me. Steaks sizzled on the barbecue and white wine chilled in the fridge. Yes, I sighed, I needed a holiday.

The days soon melted, one into the other. I took long morning walks with my new grandson, accompanied by Joanne's huge white Akita dog. Babies and dogs—both live in the moment. God, I wish I could master that, I mused. Most afternoons were spent drinking cappuccinos with friends at one of the trendy outside bistros that lined Mackenzie Avenue, Revelstoke's main street. I wished Patrick could see this transformation on Revelstoke's main drag. In Pat's day, souped up cars would lay rubber on the dusty streets and the pool hall was the only downtown attraction. A cobbled square, hanging flower baskets bursting with color, and deep red Japanese maple leaves waving in the breeze—this was not a concept in 1969.

One afternoon, a rainy drizzle hindered my usual practice of drinking java at an outdoor café so I opted to visit Patrick instead.

A cemetery conversation is one-sided, I know, but it felt natural to spend time where the only physical evidence of Patrick remained. As always, I kissed my finger and touched the *P* in "Patrick," etched in the cold gray stone. For the rest of the day, and well into the night, I felt sad and reflective.

The next morning I awoke to the soft sound of Joanne singing to Ryan, her baby son, as I lay in bed watching the sun-dappled shadows from trees dancing in the summer breeze outside my window. Then unexpectedly, a cold, icy fear enveloped my body, paralyzing me. *I was going to die.*

I'd heard of people who had suddenly taken care of all their business and later, when they died, others would say it was like he/she knew. That's how I felt, and I couldn't say a word to anyone. I had to escape this gloom, and announced to Joanne that I was leaving Revelstoke early and would go visit my father before my trip overseas.

Leaving Revelstoke's craggy, mountainous landscape behind me, the land soon softened and Shuswap Lake was now the main source of scenery. Driving through Salmon Arm, and past the turn off to Eagle Bay, I eventually crossed over to the north side of the Shuswap Lake; the sunny side, my Grandma Nelson would say. Lee Creek, Scotch Creek, and then Celista, where my Dad's home was a refuge and also my childhood home. Not much has changed in four decades. Street lights are non-existent as there are no streets; only one main road hugs the shoreline of the massive lake.

I spent the afternoons on the beach trying to shake my gloom, the same beach where my summer friend, Daphne, and I would sit on those hot summer days in the 1960s. I could almost hear our laughter and practically taste the sandwiches and icy orange Kool-Aid that we wolfed down between dunks in the cool, pristine water. Daphne, a sophisticated Vancouver city girl, was three years older than me and a lifetime wiser.

Daphne's parents were both authors, and her father was an English professor at the University of British Columbia. They probably provided me, unknowingly, an education simply by being in their presence. However, Daphne was, in my opinion, *the* authority on life. Endlessly, Daphne and her parents discussed current affairs of the early 1960s, introducing me to an outside world that I never knew existed. Daphne attended Crofton House, a private school. I was too young to be impressed by private schools, but I did love hearing about this different lifestyle. In the summer of 1964, Daphne wanted to take me to Vancouver to see a band called the *Beatles*. She said we would scream and throw jelly beans! The planned trip didn't happen, but Daphne was more disappointed than I.

That summer, we spent many warm nights sleeping on the beach that sprawled below Daphne's summer home. By the light of the moon that silhouetted the soft mountains and streaked the water with a rippling, silver glow, Daphne would triumphantly tune in her transistor radio to c-fun, a Vancouver rock station. For the first time I heard the music of the *Rolling Stones, the Dave Clark Five, the Beatles,* and *Herman's Hermits*. Daphne's favorite band was the *Dave Clark Five*. I didn't have a favorite, but chose *Herman's Hermits* to feel cool, like Daph, as I now called her.

Now, gazing across the water, I wondered what had happened to the girl I had once been, whose very soul seemed to be slipping away. Was this the final curtain call? Was my Higher Self announcing, "Okay, folks, it's a wrap?" Well, I resigned myself, maybe so. After all, everything's done. My marriage is over, the kids are grown, my search for John and Katherine is finished—all's completed. "There's nothing a cup of tea can't fix," I remembered Ros once saying.

I wondered if a cup of tea could return my soul.

That night, after a late dinner, my father and I sat on his sun deck watching the sun set over the water. Dad looked at me with concern. "Why are you going to England again? You were just there last year."

I tried to answer like a mature adult, but felt like a twelve-year-old.

"Caring for Audrey took its toll. England is home to me. I get strength there. I just need to go . . ."

My father interrupted, "You can't re-live your past life. It can't be done."

I was stunned. Dad had it all wrong and I told him so. "I'm not trying to live a past life, for God's sake, I only like going to England."

The plane slowly filled with passengers. I had settled in my seat and glanced up just in time to watch a Patrick look-alike walk by. Although the man was tall and dark, it was his slow saunter that was familiar. This was not the first time I had "seen" Patrick through the years. Patrick, or should I say, a symbol of Patrick, would often pop into my life as if to say, "Don't forget me!"

My first after-life contact from Patrick, many years after his death, had been the vivid dream during which he had said, *"Jewelle, put foxglove on my grave."* The next morning, my husband had explained to me that foxglove was a tall, spiky English flower. The message meant nothing to me and anyway, it was the remembrance of the sound of his voice that overwhelmed me. For the next three days, while the memory lasted, I savored the deep slow drawl of Patrick's voice and I cried when my brain would no longer release the sweet sound. Although I still hadn't understood his *"put foxglove on my grave"* message, I decided, literally, to do just that. On July 17, 1994, Patrick's death day, I put a single stalk of pink foxglove on his grave. It took a few more years to understand that his request had a much deeper meaning.

The Patrick look-alike disappeared into the sea of passengers at the back of the plane. I leaned back, closing my eyes, trying to fight the helplessness of feeling weak and empty as, again, the "losing my soul" feeling washed over me. I visualized a higher part of myself, whispering, "Don't go. Stay in your body. We're going home to England. We'll soon be home."

Shortly before the pilot announced our descent into Heathrow, I reached into my flight bag for my makeup bag. Along with the makeup bag came a scrap of paper that fluttered to the floor; the article that I had tucked away while still at Audrey's. I re-read the headline, *Serena* Talks to the Spirit of John Lennon*. I wondered what this American lady would think of Herma's theory—that John Lennon had, in a past life, been Branwell Brontë. If I could muster the nerve, I just may write to this psychic lady in the States, I thought, tucking the article back into my bag.

Standing in line for the small aircraft washroom, I longed for Ros' huge, old fashioned bathtub. The once spotless cubicle was now grubby from too much use. I did my best to apply makeup to a tired face, when suddenly the tiny room filled with the scent of roses. I pumped the hand soap, but no roses. I opened the garbage container—nothing. The pilot was directing us to return to our seats and fasten our seat belts. Upon opening the washroom door, the overwhelming perfume of roses dissipated and was replaced with recycled air. Too tired to ponder the mysterious incident, I returned to my seat.

After the usual tedious customs ritual, I hailed a taxi, not caring about the cost of the fifty-mile journey. Just take me home, just take me to Petworth. As I clicked on my seat belt, I could smell it. Roses! I gave the driver a lame smile while discretely checking for an air freshener, but I saw nothing.

*not her real name

The scent calmed me as I sat back on the leather seat, enjoying the trip down the M25. Turning onto a secondary motorway, my eyes, as always, filled with tears as we passed the signpost that read, *West Sussex*.

Ros welcomed me with open arms, and minutes later a knock on the door brought Ann. I had been to Petworth so many times that we had developed rituals. After several cups of steaming tea, accompanied by a plate of English biscuits, either Ann or Ros would walk me around the ancient town. This walk was not to reacquaint me with Petworth, but rather to keep me awake. My body clock said 4:00 a.m. so the wake-up walk was appreciated.

This time Ann walked with me and as we took a path overlooking the green shimmering valley I told her about the roses, or should I say the scent of roses, in the plane and cab. Ann wasn't really surprised as I usually arrived with a new puzzle to solve.

Ros and Ann lived on the same quiet cul-de-sac overlooking the rolling South Downs. Another lady, June, whom I'd met on a recent visit, also lived on the same street. Visiting June was on my to-do list after my jet lag wore off. That night, falling asleep, I felt blessed to be in the company of good friends, to rest and hopefully get myself back on track . . . and I felt blessed to be back in Petworth.

I rolled out of bed at noon feeling refreshed, and anticipating the return to all of my favorite places. I smiled when I saw the breakfast table set for me, along with a note from Ros. *Off to work—drop into the shop when you're through the town.* Ros works in a tourist gift shop in Market Square, and she knew, for the next several days, I would roam the lanes and countryside until my thirst for all of my old haunts had been quenched.

As always, as if seeing Petworth for the first time, I drank in every detail. I started with a walk through a dark, hedged alley leading to Rosemary Garden, a miniature park where mothers took their small children and the elderly rested on wooden benches. The park led to a lane and also to the entrance of Golden Square, which led to Market Square, the centre of Petworth. Golden Square was where I had first seen myself, three hundred years ago, in a past life regression. Market Square is a busy conglomerate of shoppers and traffic. Across the square is quiet, dignified Lombard Street, an ancient cobblestoned lane that has seen 800 years of Petworth life. On a trip, years earlier, I had the sudden urge to skip down this street. I could feel myself as a young girl who skipped daily along these cobblestones. I looked down at my middle-aged body, dressed in jeans and a sweater, and repressed the urge! Instead, I continued walking towards St. Mary's Church which loomed in the distance.

My past life as Katherine James never ceased to fascinate me, and as I wandered through the cemetery of St. Mary's, I wondered what Katherine would think of Jewelle. I felt so close to Katherine, even protective of her. Years and years ago, I knew, I just *knew* that Katherine had been 17 when she died, and I also just knew she was buried here. Later, this information was verified by the Records Office. Katherine James had died at the age of 17, was *"buried in wool"* on May 23, 1683, and was laid to rest at St. Mary's. Looking across the lawn, dotted with illegible headstones, I said a prayer for Katherine and for John.

I completely absorbed my surroundings. The roof tops of Petworth were of different angles of gabled and thatched structures, all vying for space. A 15th Century inn was now a private home, while a Tudor hotel having proudly endured the centuries, was now a tea shop. Small alleys and courtyards could be found, but not easily seen from the High Street. Buildings with low doorways and tiny windows were not uncommon. Chiseled into stone walls were the years 1653 or 1780, all reminders of yesterday.

I popped into a bakery to purchase a late lunch to go; a sausage roll, a scone with jam, and a Ribena to drink. Before heading out to the country, I stopped at Ros' shop. We both laughed when she saw my lunch. Ros knew that part of my absorbing the surroundings was to eat all of the old-style British delicacies I could. Not only was the food delicious, but a reminder of lives spent here. Sussex cake, mincemeat, ginger beer, and meat pies all brought back memories.

Ros' tiny shop suddenly filled with European tourists. I waved goodbye and ran across the square, up Lombard Street, around a corner entering Barton's Lane, leading to the valley. Hard to believe, but the peaceful, green valley that lay in the distance was only blocks from the busy town centre.

I recalled my visit to the valley with Becky, five years earlier. Ann's psychic daughter had met with me that memorable September morning with the specific purpose of psychically feeling the emotions of Katherine and John. It was when we started walking along the path that overlooked the valley that Becky had to suddenly sit down. Becky's knees were weak, and her eyes had filled with tears. The valley, three hundred years later, still held the loss, the emotion, and the pain, of the two lovers parting.

The memory of that morning was as vivid as yesterday. As I sat on the bench that overlooked the valley, I knew, for the rest of my life, I would return here again and again. Gazing across the rolling, green landscape, I half expected a man with shoulder length, sandy colored hair to emerge over the horizon.

"I miss you, John Baron," I whispered.

Moments later a plane from nearby Gatwick Airport flew overhead, bringing me back to the present. Once again, I felt my soul struggling to escape from my body.

Twenty-three

I felt lightheaded as I forced myself to leave the bittersweet scene of the valley and began to walk back to Ros' home. Instead of unlocking Ros' door, I knocked on her neighbor's instead. June, whom I'd met at my book signing party last year, had given me an open invitation to pop in for tea and a visit anytime. A golden lab and June greeted me. "June, it's me, Jewelle."

June looked pleased. "Oh, do come in," she said, and we hugged warmly. I followed June into her sitting room, her golden lab a step ahead of us.

"You're back," June patted my hand. "But why so soon? It's been only what, eight months since your book party? It's wonderful, of course, to have you here, dear, but what's wrong?"

Tears sprang to my eyes, but I knew only my voice would convince June that all was well. "I just needed a holiday," I smiled, forcing my voice to be light, "and you know me, where else would I go? Too much has happened this year. In one year I moved to another town, became divorced, published a book, and my last job was, well, it's been quite a time."

"And you needed to come home," June stated.

"Yes," I gulped. I didn't mention that my soul was also trying to make it's great escape. June and the golden lab looked sympathetic, but only the lab witnessed my tears because June is blind.

"We need a cuppa," June announced and left the room. When she returned with a tray of tea and home-made cookies, I felt ashamed of myself. Here was a woman who had overcome adversities in life, much greater than any I had encountered, and I was the one crying.

I recalled when I first noticed June's interested face in the audience at the book party. When a series of questions were asked of me, hers was unusual and thought provoking. June's voice was clear. "Jewelle, is your birthday the same day as Katherine James'?"

In my book I had written that Katherine had been christened on February 24, 1666. Later, after the party, I did some research and discovered that a child was christened, in those days, within a two-week period after her birth. This would, indeed, put Katherine's birthday close or even exactly on my birthday of February 12th—a connection that had never occurred to me. June would know neither of these bits of information as she had not read my book and never would. I was endeared to her that, even though she was blind, she took an interest in a story she could only hear of from others.

"June," I said, "I'll be in Petworth for the summer. Would you like me to read *Just Imagine* to you?"

June's face glowed. "I would love it!" She became thoughtful. "Could we wait for a few days? I would like to record it; I'll need to get a machine."

I promised to return in a few days.

That night, after fish and chips for tea, Ros showed me three tickets.

"On Saturday night, we're going to a picnic and musical festival at the park."

The park was Petworth Park, the picnic was like no picnic I

had ever been on, and the night of music returned my soul. Later, I wrote to my cousin, Dayle, all about the evening.

Dayle is more than my cousin, Dayle is my mother's best friend. As a child, I would eavesdrop on their many conversations on spiritual matters. Dayle would tell us of her yearly mystical journeys to Ireland, and she would bring us gifts; pewter leprechauns and once, a four-leaf clover, picked from a field where the fairies danced—or so I had imagined. Dayle makes people feel special and important, a quality that, I'm sure, endeared her to her students through her years as a school teacher. This same quality gave me the courage to share my past life search with her. Over two decades and through hundreds of letters, I have shared with Dayle the ups and downs of my journey into the past. With endless patience, Dayle explained to me what I was experiencing.

"Life is a pattern," she would write, "and we repeat and repeat our lives and their lessons until we get it right." Dayle insisted that our individual responsibility lies in recognizing and unravelling the intricate design of our lives, both past and present. "The Universe," she would say, "is a power station of love, and love is all you need to overcome the negative working of the ego." "Love is the real world," Dayle would write in huge flowing letters, using her teacher's red pen, hoping I would get the message! So, as I have always done, I wrote to Dayle.

Dear Dayle,

Greetings from England; ah, it's good to be home. I'm writing, while it's still fresh in my mind, of a picnic last night in the park. The park was Petworth Park, on the grounds of Petworth House.

There were thousands (yes, thousands) of people spread out on the lawns, covering every inch of the grounds. And did I say picnic? I know you're conjuring up a Canadian picnic—a blanket on the ground and sandwiches to eat. This English picnic was, picture this, groups of people sitting at tables which were covered with white linen tablecloths, champagne chilling in wine buckets, silver trays of choco-late-covered strawberries, candles in gothic style candlestick holders, and bouquets of roses. My mouth is still open, thinking about it! I "picnicked" with Ros, her husband, John, and their friends, although they weren't as posh as the champagne sippers. We did have, however, food galore, wine flowing, laughter, and dancing all night long.

Dayle, the best was yet to come! The band was some distance across the grounds but, when they struck a few chords, I was pretty sure who they were.

"Ros, is that, uh, no, it can't be!" I hesitated, because I had assumed the band was a local one.

Ros had laughed. "This is a local band, after all, they are British."

"Herman's Hermits!" I squealed, grabbing my camera. I could hear Ros laughing as I ran through the crowd, eventually inching my way to the front of the stage. The songs that Daphne and I had lis-tened to on the beach, through her transistor radio, were now playing only feet away. The Hermits were older now, of course, but they sounded the same, and for a split second I felt it—my soul was with me completely.

Dayle, it was such a night, and at midnight everyone sang Rule Britannia and waved their Union Jacks. I was utterly and blissfully happy to stand amongst the crowd, and feel their love for Britain.

Love,
Jewelle

Only after posting the letter did I realize that I hadn't explained to Dayle about the comment concerning my soul. This slip-up if revealed to anyone else would have been embarrassing, but to Dayle I knew it would be all right. Also, in my haste to share with Dayle our picnic in the park, I had forgotten to tell her of the scent of roses on my journey over the pond. I purchased a postcard, choosing a scene of thatched cottages of Sussex, and wrote in the limited space.

Dayle,

On the plane, as we were landing at Heathrow, I could smell roses (in the stale washroom) and an hour later, the same scent was in a (smoking) taxi. It reminded me of the lavender.

Love,

J

Ah, yes, I remembered—the lavender experiment. In the summer of 1992, I purchased a bundle of beautiful dried lavender tied in a purple ribbon. I had decided that if a scent could trigger a memory from our childhood, such as the scent of sun tan lotion taking us to a beach somewhere, then maybe a scent could recall a past life memory as well.

Holding the bundle of lavender, I lay on the bed, closed my eyes, and gently waved the dried flowers below my nose. *Instantly, I was hurled back in time observing the scene before me. John Baron and I were in a room, but we weren't the John and Katherine from Petworth, we were in another time. I slowly observed the room, starting at one end and meticulously took in every detail. The rich wood furniture was heavy, the walls were adorned with tapestries, and the windows were covered in white lace. John was watching nervously through the windows to the outside, as if expecting enemies. Then, I saw it—a baby's cradle, and folded on a table nearby, a white baby's cap and a long, white christening gown. The cradle was empty.*

I screamed at John, "Where's the baby?" He didn't answer, but continued watching the window for enemies or intruders.

I put down the lavender and opened my eyes. My head throbbed. The lavender scent was nauseating, and I threw the bundle out the window.

Dayle would remember the lavender experience, although

she wasn't sure about my memories, only that they were obviously from the past. She would also recall how I had developed a deep cough the next day. Throughout the remainder of that summer, the cough, now deep in my chest, was beginning to worry me. By September, two months later, I consulted a doctor. I was scared. The doctor listened to my chest and my breathing, reporting all was well. By the time I returned home the cough was gone, never to return. However, the lingering memory of John and me in a beautiful room with an empty baby cradle was, and still is, haunting.

I popped the postcard to Dayle, mentioning roses and lavender, into a red mailbox. Purchasing more postcards, I wrote home saying that I missed everyone, which was true, but quite honestly I could stay here forever, settling into a cottage tucked away amongst the many winding lanes.

My father's words rang in my head, "Jewelle, you can't re-live a past life. It can't be done."

Petworth life, that summer, continued in a comfortable routine. I spent the days wandering and absorbing the green countryside, the hedges, the abundant flowers, the stone and brick buildings, and let the surroundings flow through me, feeding my soul. Many afternoons I spent with June, reading *Just Imagine* into her tape recorder, while June's lab would sit at my feet.

One early morning, Ann called. "You must see Becky for a reading."

Ann was right—a reading from Becky was one of my Petworth rituals. For me, Becky's readings are a visit from John. Of all the psychics I've encountered, Becky seems to connect herself with John. It's like John knows her personally, making a reading clear and true.

Petworth, at dusk, has a pink hue surrounding the town, accentuating the vivid colors of flowers in pots and baskets and in gardens and window boxes. One such early evening, Becky and I sat in Ann's English garden.

"All afternoon my hand has been tingling, which it often does when a spirit is preparing to speak," Becky said.

Since our first meeting, years ago, Becky had further developed her psychic abilities, and was now referring to automatic writing. The first time I watched Becky's pen flow, with words that were often in rhyme, I was amazed at the speed of her pen on paper.

The words now began to write. *"Hello, Becky. Hello, Julia."* (A reading from John, through Becky, often begins with him referring to me as Julia.)

"I have been watching you, Julia. I am so happy you have come back to Petworth. So many memories are here, this is us, this is our place. I know, Julia, that you're not sure which direction, in your life, to take. Just follow the clouds, Katherine, and follow your heart. Your answers lie within, for only you to discover. I am waiting in the wings, but not far away. Our past life together is not your imagination, it is real. Katherine, you were with child."

Abruptly Becky's pen stopped, and she gasped, "Someone else is in the room! A young man; he's dark, tall, and he's angry. He's just stormed in . . ."

Becky picked up her pen again. This time the words were written in a jerking fashion.

"You gave up our son. You didn't want him; he was part of me so you mustn't have loved me."

I looked at Becky and simply said, "Patrick." Then, a wave of emotion from twenty years ago washed over me, and I began to cry.

"Tell him," I said to Becky, my voice shaking, "that he's a jerk. A great big jerk!"

Becky was silent as I repeated, "Tell him."

"I think he heard you," Becky said softly.

I began to rant, but didn't care. "Then, if he's listening, I have a few things to say. I would have married you, Patrick, if you had asked me. I gave up our son because I had to. I did the best I could. No one offered to help find a way to keep him, and certainly not you, Patrick White!" I was choking with frustration and then, a second later, I felt calm again.

"Patrick is calm as well," Becky said, as words flowed once again from her pen.

"I just don't want you to forget me. We both need healing."

"Blimey," June murmured the next day, as I told her of my reading with Becky.

"Yeah," I smiled. "Becky commented later that she'd never had a spirit come through all angry and feisty. Most spirits are happy to be communicating with their loved ones."

"And what about John calling you Julia?"

"When I was born, my parents named me Julia. That only lasted for ten days though, and I was never registered as Julia. Only my parents and I know this. And John obviously knows, too."

"And what about Katherine being with child?"

"I don't know, but I'll keep this info tucked away. Maybe I'll find an answer in the future."

An envelope, addressed to me, popped through Ros' mail slot—a cheque from a local book store. "The Universe does provide;" Moira's words rang in my head.

By that afternoon, I had booked a short holiday to Scotland with the book store money. Dumping my flight bag of its contents, I began to repack for the trip. The ad, with the headline, *Serena Speaks to the Spirit of John Lennon*, once again came to my attention.

"Just do it," I scolded myself, "write to this lady."

The Scotland-bound tour bus inched its way through Sussex, stopping at towns and villages until eventually every seat was filled. Except for the bus driver, I was the only passenger who had dark hair and was under the age of fifty. The group of senior citizens was a quiet lot, and I appreciated this time to be alone with my thoughts.

The first night we spent in Leeds, Yorkshire, a rough industrial city. All was unfamiliar and for the first time all summer, I felt like a tourist. The next day, I was thrilled as any foreigner to be greeted at Scotland's border by a Scotsman, complete with a tartan kilt and playing the bagpipes. Traveling through a series of small towns, we arrived at nightfall at our destination, Callender, in Rob Roy Country.

After settling into our gothic-style hotel, I knew that in order to enjoy myself the matter of the ad must be dealt with. I felt vulnerable, as in my early days of searching, to once again lay my heart on the table and say, "Here's my story," especially to a woman who speaks to John. What if Serena thinks I'm all wrong? Come on, Jewelle, be honest with yourself. What you're thinking is, what if John says you're all wrong? Yeah, that was it. Despite all that I'd discovered, I was afraid to contact Serena, the lady who channels John Lennon. Then, like jumping into a cold lake, or should I say "loch," I found a mailbox, and for better or worse posted the letter to America.

For the next several days I absorbed every detail of Callender and the nearby surroundings. Red-haired lassies danced the highland fling, young men strolled down the main street in kilts, and I often heard the haunting sound of bagpipes echoed through the soft hills, creating a mystical mood.

We visited Sterling Castle, a beautiful and daunting fortress that stood high on a hill. It was easy to visualize enemies unable to climb the castle walls. Touring the craggy countryside, one half expected to see Liam Neeson, our modern association of Rob Roy, emerge.

One afternoon, the tour bus driver took us on a journey through the Scottish lowlands. The driver explained that we were too early in the summer to enjoy the heather, but he hoped we liked the wild foxglove.

My surroundings became surreal. Most of the elderly passengers fell asleep, lulled perhaps, by the hypnotic ballads playing on the bus' sound system. We were floating down a narrow roadway, surrounded by a sea of foxglove. Tall purple, pink, and white stalks waved in the summer breeze. *"Heal, heal,"* the waving foxglove seemed to say. Suddenly, the bus stopped at a tea shop nestled in this wilderness. After having a cup of strong milky tea and fingers of shortbread, I thumbed through a rack of postcards. One postcard, depicting a sea of foxglove, caught my eye. Turning the card over, I was shocked to read, *Foxglove—a drug, digitalis, to heal the heart, is derived from foxglove.* "To heal the heart." The words drummed in my head. My dream of Patrick came to mind, with his voice urging me, *"Jewelle, put foxglove on my grave,"* and the words, through Becky's pen, from Patrick, *"We both need healing."* Just an hour earlier, the words, *"Heal, heal,"* came to my mind as the wild foxglove waved in the wind. Then John who had said, also through Becky's pen, *"Follow your heart, Katherine."*

I knew what I had to do—to heal my heart, to heal with Patrick. There was unfinished business in this life. My past life would always be waiting, but my present life meant returning to Revelstoke.

The last night, before returning to England, was spent walking Callander's only main street. The Scottish air, clear and crisp like British Columbia's, was filled with the romantic strains of the bagpipes. I finally knew what the future held. I had to return to Canada to heal old wounds. I felt like a kid re-turning to school in September; not knowing what the year ahead would bring, only knowing that I must show up for class.

The day before I left Petworth, I went to visit June. We had made arrangements earlier to go on a walk-about.

"Where would you like to go, June?" I smiled affectionately at her.

"Oh," she said, thoughtfully, "let's just walk."

June's golden lab looked sad. "Don't worry," June had sensed her dog's mood. "Jewelle will take care of me. You stay here and rest."

When June and I stepped onto the sidewalk, I offered her my arm. June jumped at my touch, startling both of us. She laughed. "Oh, you *are* real."

"Of course, I'm real!" I joined in her laughter.

"You'll think me daft, but when you first came to visit, earlier this summer, I couldn't feel your presence. After you had left, I mentioned to my husband that I didn't know if you had been here or not."

He thought I was mad and said, "Of course, Jewelle was here."

June's face became serious. "But really, I couldn't sense your soul, like you were a shell or an apparition."

"Oh, my God, June," I breathed in sharply, "just before leaving Canada, I could feel my soul slipping away. It was terrifying and I couldn't share it with anyone."

"But now," June patted my hand, "you are back. I can feel a whole being beside me."

Yes, bit by bit this summer, my soul had been fed by the beauty of Sussex, the warmth of friends, and I had been given further instructions on the next chapter of my life—to go home and heal with Patrick.

June and I walked the lanes, enjoying the warm sunshine and

the scent of flowers. We later drank lemonade and ate chocolate cake at a tea shop on Lombard Street. It had been a good day and a good summer.

I was finishing my packing when I heard Ros' phone ring in two short successions, the way British phones do.

"Jewelle, it's for you," Ros called.

Worried that something was wrong at home, I flew down the stairs. The voice was American, not Canadian.

"This is Serena." *The American lady who channels John Lennon!*

I was breathless. "Serena. Hello, thank you for calling."

"I received your letter and felt compelled to call you in England."

Remembering that this woman had spoken to John for years through channeling made me suddenly shy.

Serena asked, "You feel you've lived a past life with John Lennon?"

"Aaahh, yes, I believe I have," I said, staring out the window at the rolling South Downs, "not as John Lennon, obviously, but a man named John Baron, a man in the 1600s, who I believe was John Lennon from an earlier life."

"You're Canadian?" Serena asked.

"Yes, actually I'm just packing to leave for home. I've been here for most of the summer." My mind was racing. Here was a woman who channels John, and I couldn't think of a word to say.

As if reading my mind, Serena said, "John wants you to know that Emily Brontë is his favorite poet."

"Emily Brontë," I tried to keep my voice level, "why isn't that interesting? She's my favorite as well." I wanted to jump up and down and shout, "Guess what? My friend Herma psychically saw that John was Emily's brother, Branwell, in another life!" Instead, I offered to send Serena a copy of *Just Imagine* and in turn, she promised to write to me in Canada.

After hanging up the phone, I told Ros that I was going out for a bit. I had one last goodbye to say. A light rain fell as I sat on a bench overlooking the valley. Although every trip to England ended with a vow to return, today's promise was different.

Closing my eyes and breathing in the Sussex air, I made a pact with my soul. In my next life, I would be re-born here in Petworth. A warm calm engulfed me, and I opened my eyes just in time to see a little girl, with dark, bouncing curls, skipping towards me. I wondered why she was here alone, when I was startled with an understanding. The little girl was a symbol, clinching my pact to be re-born here. As she skipped by, our eyes met for a second and I knew I'd just seen my future.

Twenty-four

Beautiful British Columbia, I thought as, a few days later I drove across the Columbia River Bridge into Revelstoke. While in Scotland, my message to return and heal had been crystal clear and now a further explanation drummed in my head.

My inner voice whispered, "This is school. Revelstoke is your classroom. You cannot skip class as there is much to learn."

"I am a pupil?" I challenged this inner voice of mine.

"Yes."

"And who is the teacher?" I asked.

"You."

"I'm the teacher *and* the pupil? This should be interesting."

However, deep inside I knew that all was not right in my world so I knew I had work to do. Fifteen years ago, I had one simple question. Why did John Lennon's death upset me so much? The question, when finally answered, should have brought me peace and understanding, or so I had expected. But enlightened I was not, and still there were missing pieces to the puzzle. And were these pieces here in Revelstoke? My only clues were words from John, through Becky. *"Follow your heart,*

Katherine. I am waiting in the wings;" and clues from waving fox-glove that whispered, "H*eal, heal."*

The phone rang. It was Moira. Would I like to accompany her on a road trip to Southern Alberta? I viewed the contents of my new apartment—open boxes everywhere, my Beatles poster ready for hanging, and clothes scattered about. I decided, like any other student, that one last summer adventure before September would postpone the inevitable classroom time.

Moira arrived the next morning and we were soon heading east in her Jeep. Moira drove while Casey, her cocker spaniel, and I vied for position in the passenger seat.

Moira looked happy and peaceful. We hadn't seen each other since I had cared for Audrey. Moira filled me in on her life. Her reputation as a trusted psychic was growing, and next month she would be leaving for England, to Stanstead College, to take courses in spiritual growth and development.

For a while, we traveled in silence. The Rogers Pass was at the height of its beauty this Labour Day weekend. The rugged mountains, dusted with the year's first snowfall, surrounded us while bright yellow aspen trees swaying against blue skies provided a smorgasbord of autumn color.

Unexpectedly, Moira blurted, "Tell me about Patrick!"

"Patrick?"

"I re-read *Just Imagine* this summer, and I knew you only touched on your feelings for Patrick."

"Patrick," I mused, absentmindedly scratching the spaniel's ears. "This very highway is the road that brought me to Revelstoke, at age 16. After leaving the North Shuswap, our family moved to Field, in Yoho National Park."

"What would teenagers do in Field?" Moira asked.

"All that is wholesome," I smiled.

"And at age 16 you moved to Revelstoke?"

"Yes, to me, it was a swinging city. The girls were hip and the guys were tough. *American Graffiti* could easily have been set in Revelstoke, in 1969. Here, I met the James Dean of them all; Patrick White, nicknamed Skid."

The first time I laid eyes on him he just grinned and grinned, like the Cheshire Cat. I laughed in remembrance. My memories came flooding back, and Moira couldn't have stopped me talking about Patrick if she'd tried.

"Skid was brilliant," I said. "He was able to attend school when he felt like it, and still pull off straight As. Skid's roots, on his father's side were Irish and from there he got his personality; charming, witty, and affectionate. I had never known anyone like him and I still don't. To me, he was the coolest of the cool, except for the time we went skiing."

"You ski?" Moira asked.

"In those days, I did. Skiing was *the* wholesome activity in Field. One night a group of us went night skiing at Revelstoke's Mt. Mackenzie."

"Patrick skied?"

"No," I burst out laughing. "If Patrick White had ever been on a pair of skis, you'd never have known it. Here came *Mr. Cool* flying down the hill, arms and legs flailing, his body completely out of control. Unbeknownst to Patrick, that was the moment I fell in love with him."

We were still laughing as Moira pulled the Jeep into a parking lot beside a roadside café near Golden. Moira took Casey for a much needed walk as I entered the café and chose a booth. A group of laughing teenagers at the next table brought back more memories.

Sally Ann's Coffee Shop—Revelstoke's teen hangout. The place to be. Here at Sally's, while sipping a cola and sharing a booth with five other girls, did I learn the story behind Patrick's nickname, Skid. The story was legend by the time I heard it.

The original Skid had been Michael White, Patrick's adored, older brother. Michael had died instantly in a car accident in the summer of 1967, devastating Patrick. I never did hear Patrick mention his brother, but later when we were closer I noticed the evidence of his pain; an unprofessional blue tattoo on his upper arm that read *SKID II*.

As Moira appeared I hid my face behind a menu wiping away a tear; then faking perkiness I announced I was starving.

The next few days, Moira and I were tourists as well as salesladies. Stopping at New Age shops and bookstores in small mountain towns and through the Crowsnest Pass, Moira would do psychic readings, while I sold copies of *Just Imagine*. We indulged ourselves with high tea at the Prince of Wales Hotel in Waterton National Park, and drove to Montana, just to say we'd been there. We ended our road trip by sitting on the banks of the Oldman River, near Pincher Creek, with a bottle of the Okanagan's finest chilled white wine.

The sun was beginning to set behind the dry brown hills that overlooked the lazy river. We sat where generations of Blackfoot Indians had roamed the hills, hunting buffalo and fishing.

Moira asked, "How did you and Patrick end?"

I threw a rock into the slow moving water. "The first time we ended, I left town."

"Why did you leave?"

I can still hear the phone ringing—a pale green phone, a chic color in 1970, and the doctor's voice telling me the test was positive; a baby was due in the autumn.

"Patrick was to pick me up at the ice cream parlour where I worked. I had my pregnant speech all prepared, but he never showed up."

I fell silent. The cocker spaniel licked my hand as if to say, "It's okay, keep talking."

"Arrangements were made for me to leave town. I never told

Patrick that I was pregnant; the grapevine took care of that." Tears were flowing down my cheeks. "I felt jilted, like he didn't care. And if he didn't care, then neither did I."

"Looks like you still do care," Moira said softly.

"Patrick was 19, and I was 17, the night I took a Greyhound to Saskatoon. A family disgrace, I was. The plan was I would live with a rich family on a grain farm, who needed a girl to work in the house. The family was good to me. I ate well, had my own room, and when my jeans became too tight, the lady took me shopping for maternity clothes. The lady also took me to the welfare office in Saskatoon, to start the adoption process for my baby."

"Adoption," Moira said, "the only solution for young, single, pregnant women in those days."

"After a time, when the baby grew inside me and became more real, I came up with a plan. The house where I worked was large, as was my room; perhaps I could keep the baby and continue to work for them? The lady said I could stay, if I wished, but not the baby.

"There was no one else to turn to and I felt so alone. I began to detest the hot, dusty prairie. There were no lakes nearby, no swimming or waterskiing, and no picnics on the beach. Even at night, the air blew hot. There was no cool mountain air to breathe.

"One late afternoon in August, I left the farm. It was harvest time and the lady had taken supper out to the men who were working in the wheat fields. I threw my clothes in a suitcase, and started walking down the flat dirt road, hoping to escape before I was discovered missing." Despite my memories, I had to laugh.

"Moira, what a sight I must have been! A teenaged girl, nearly seven month's pregnant, struggling with a bulky suitcase. A farmer in a tractor came along, and into his cab I went for the ten-mile journey to the nearest bus depot.

"Weeks earlier, while at the welfare office, I had seen a poster describing *Bethany Home for Unwed Mothers*. By nightfall, I stood at the door of the enormous stone gothic-style building and rang the bell.

"While on the farm, I had been an oddity to the neighbors and was often referred to as "the girl from B.C." Suddenly, in Bethany Home, I had sisters all around me; pregnant teens, scared, but still wanting to be happy despite their predicament. One night a dozen of us very pregnant girls waddled across a crosswalk on our way to a movie. The stares from the drivers of cars, as we paraded in front of them, were priceless. We killed ourselves laughing, and it felt so good to belong again.

"The Bethany Home was run by the Salvation Army and had religious overtones. The trade-off was we went to chapel twice a day, did light chores, and behaved ourselves because after all, we *had* sinned; our bodies showed the evidence.

"Late at night, we girls traded stories and they were all similar. The Bethany Home would not allow us to exchange surnames and strangely, because we could have secretly revealed our identities, we never did. Through the years, I've wondered about a girl from Regina, named Melanie.

"Twice a day, sitting in the chapel, I stared at the phone booth in the hallway as bouts of homesickness often washed over me. I began to save my quarters and one night I called Sally Ann's Coffee Shop. Yes, Skid was there."

"Babe," he drawled, and I knew he was stoned. Sure he would send money; yes, he knew about our child. Queen Street in Saskatoon? Sure, he'd send a cheque right away. The money I didn't need, but a connection with Patrick I did need. After hanging up the phone, I felt more alone than ever.

"One by one, the girls left for the hospital which was conveniently located right across the street from our stone home. Returning days later, with flat stomachs, it was their changed dispositions I noticed; all were quiet and subdued. My time, I knew, was also coming near. The welfare people happily informed me that a home had been chosen for my child. No details of the parents and their lifestyle were provided, so I could only guess. Probably, they lived on a farm somewhere in rural Saskatchewan, at least five miles from the nearest neighbor. The winters would be cold and biting, but no skiing. The summers would be hot and dusty, but no swimming.

"The next morning, at breakfast, yet another girl returned from the hospital. I visualized her child already on his way to his new prairie home. It all became too much. As I had done leaving the farm, I now bolted from Saskatoon. I felt my life depended on safely boarding the Greyhound and leaving the prairie. Only when, the next day, the snow-capped Rocky Mountains loomed in the distance, did I breathe a sigh of relief.

"Our child, a boy, as fate would have, was born in British Columbia a week later.

"And that," I declared to Moira, "is how it ended for Patrick and me. At least for a few years."

Twenty-five

Two uneventful weeks had passed since Moira and I returned from Alberta.

Unemployment insurance took care of my bank account, while family and friends made life stable. If only I could do something about my hair, I thought, staring critically into the mirror. I randomly chose a hair salon and met Cindy, the stylist. Cindy laughed when I told her that my hair was all wrong and I couldn't fix it.

"Yes," she said knowingly, "most comments by customers concerning their hair are really just reflections on one's life."

I stared at her in the mirror. Was she a hairdresser or a psychiatrist?

"Same thing," Cindy chuckled. "Everything we see and the way we perceive the world is just a reflection of where we are emotionally."

"Hey," she said, in a sudden revelation, "you're Jewelle Lewis. I loved your book! I knew the name "Jewelle" was familiar."

I had just made a new friend. "And you are Cindy . . . ?"

"Powell. Cindy Powell."

Strange, because her name was also familiar although I couldn't place why.

That night I received a call from a friend of a friend. Would I be interested in a waitressing job? I wasn't sure if this was my first classroom assignment or a gift from the Universe, but I accepted the employment offer whatever it meant.

The restaurant was an environment which I had to adjust quickly in order to survive. Fast pace, smoky blue air, short-tempered cooks, and truckers telling dirty jokes are some memories which come to mind.

Morning shift meant waking up before the crack of dawn, my eyes burning from lack of sleep, and arriving at a dark restaurant, where for several hours I would pour endless cups of coffee. "What in hell is this?" I asked my calm inner self, who had guided me here to this so-called school. However, night shift was a different world. The bosses were gone and we did our own thing. The night cook, Kathy, and I became friends. I nicknamed her *Mrs. Bridges* as she reminded me of the cook, Mrs. Bridges, from the 1970s British TV series, *Upstairs, Downstairs*. Like the TV show's Mrs. Bridges, Kathy ran the kitchen "tickedy-boo," and heaven help the young employees who slacked off. In between customers and orders, Kathy listened to my English stories and indulged me in my reminiscing of beautiful green Sussex.

One night the radio, which played constantly, caught my attention—*Crazy Love* by Van Morrison. My eyes blurred with tears.

"What?" Kathy looked startled.

"That song brings Patrick right here." I waved my hand around the waitress' station and repeated, "Right here, beside me."

An airmail letter arrived from Serena, the John Lennon channeler, my new friend from the States. Our telephone conversation as I was leaving Petworth, now seemed a distant memory, except for Serena's statement, *"John says Emily Brontë is his favourite poet."* I remembered wanting so badly to tell her how my friend, Herma, had seen that Emily's brother, Branwell, had been a previous life of John Lennon's. I was still proud of myself for biting my tongue, especially when I read Serena's letter.

I was intrigued by Serena's psychic gift. Maybe she could answer a question for me. I explained that in other channeled messages that I'd received from Judy, John had said, *"Yes, Katherine and Jewelle are the same, as I am John Baron or actually it was John the Baron of York descent."* Since Serena had channeled John, perhaps she could shed some light on John's statement, *"I am John the Baron of York decent."* I could almost hear Serena's southern drawl as I began to read.

Dear Jewelle,

Jewelle, to answer your question of "John the Baron of York descent"—the War of Roses, 1470, the York rose was white and Lancashire had the red rose, so John the Baron of York would have a white rose on his crest and shield.

John Lennon told me that the white rose was his ancient family's rose.

Jewelle, I've tuned into John's spirit, to ask what he thinks of John's and Katherine's life together in Petworth. This is the response I get.

"The answer is to accept that what the spirit has informed you is correct. Your lives were as stated, don't question facts. John and Katherine, the music, the dancing, all belong to that life together. As do John and Emily Brontë."

John and Emily Brontë. The answer is a simple one. In one of John's past lives he was Branwell Brontë. This is the reason he brought Emily into your life and mine.

Love,
Serena

My heart pounded and my hands were shaking as I scrawled a note to Dayle . . .

. . . remember when, years ago, my friend, Herma, had a vision that John Lennon had been Emily Brontë's brother, Branwell? I <u>just</u> received a letter from Serena, my new psychic friend in the States, who channels John. Serena told me exactly the same information—that John had been Branwell.

I am speechless!

Love,

J

I quickly scrawled another note, this time to Serena.

Dear Serena,

Thank you for your messages from John.

I am a person who needs verification (of spirit messages) in the form of tangible proof. Years ago, locating "my own birth record in 1666" was proof (to me) of my earlier life.

Serena, John has given you the exact information that I received seven years ago from a friend—that John Lennon (in a past incarnation) had been Branwell Brontë.

This is my kind of proof!

Thank you, again.

Love,

Jewelle

Twenty-six

For weeks, I coasted as many of us do—eating, sleeping, working. So, why the thought struck me like an electric shock, I have no idea. All I know is that when it came, in a mind-blowing second, it could not be disregarded or even ignored. *John and Katherine. Patrick and Jewelle.* The lives were the same; it was the same story, or very close.

As if in slow motion, I turned off the phone, fluffed a pillow, and prepared for a day's reading. I began to read my own story, *Just Imagine*, looking at the whole scenario from a view I had never thought of before.

I began to read; the radio DJ in December, 1980, announcing the shocking news that John Lennon had been shot. My memories went to an earlier radio broadcast in the summer of 1974 in Revelstoke. I had been driving down a nondescript street that ran parallel to the railway tracks. My car was white, the time was 9:00 a.m., the sun was shining; these minute details are etched in my mind. I turned on the radio to catch the news.

"Patrick Brian White, age 23, of Revelstoke, was killed instantly last night when the vehicle he was driving skidded out of control, hitting a B.C. Hydro truck."

Dead. Skid was *dead*. I felt sick. It couldn't be. We have things to settle. We're not finished yet.

The days to follow were a blur. I remember phoning Pat's friends, Tom and Sheila, in Invermere, and sharing the bad news. Later, I offered to babysit their daughter while they attended Patrick's funeral. I could not face saying goodbye to Skid; babysitting was my way out.

Two years later, on a cold November afternoon, I sought out Patrick's grave for the first time. I just needed to see it. I stood there for a very long time and finally, through blurred tears, I kissed my finger and gently touched the *P* for "Patrick," engraved in the cold stone. I didn't realize this gesture would become my ritual through the years.

In July, 1973, a year before Patrick's death, I attended a dance with my new husband. The enormous civic centre was full, the live band was playing, and my husband and I sat at one of the many tables surrounding the dance floor. Out of nowhere came Patrick and he was asking me to dance. My husband scowled in much the same way Katherine's father had when John Baron had whisked her away.

I hadn't seen Skid for so long, yet when his arms were around me time ceased to exist and all was so familiar. One dance led to another, and I smiled at him fondly for I knew that dancing wasn't his favorite sport. My memories are crystal clear. The room was becoming hot and the lights were low. A gentle waltz played. Ever so slightly, Patrick moved his face next to mine and he whispered, "Can I see you sometime?"

Reality hit. I was a married woman, no longer a teenager. My soul longed to say "yes," but I heard my voice say, "I can't. I'm sorry, I just cannot."

In slow motion, it seemed, I watched him walk away through the laughing crowd quickly fading from my sight. I wanted to scream for him to return, but the words were frozen in my throat.

I was coming to the end of *Just Imagine*. I read about Katherine being held prisoner in the attic room. Just a few months ago Becky had said, through John's words, Katherine had been *with child*. I'd often wondered why the James family would allow Katherine to be shut away. Well, I thought cynically, an unmarried, pregnant daughter is a disgrace no matter what century! I recalled my "great escape" from Saskatoon in 1970. My fears had seemed a bit dramatic, yet I felt that my life, and the life of my child, depended on my getting away. I wondered if there was a past-life connection with all of these feelings.

I closed *Just Imagine* and grabbed my coat. I needed to walk, I needed to think. Walking to downtown Revelstoke was a walk down memory lane. Patrick's family home, once a rambling weather-beaten house, was now a renovated, sterile blue-painted building, complete with skylights and a manicured lawn. Sally Ann's coffee shop was no longer the hangout, instead a music shop occupied the premises. It seemed that all the old buildings were renovated and now labelled *Heritage*. Even a certain house on Mackenzie Avenue, I smiled to myself. Once a dilapidated party house (where Patrick first kissed me), it was now sided with brick and surrounded by a cobblestone patio. Beautiful hanging flower baskets of assorted colors hung about, and amongst the cobblestones were plaques dating the house's renovations. I was feeling like a heritage relic myself with my decades' old memories!

A car pulled up beside me, parking directly in front of the building. I noticed a huge cardboard box in the back seat that was pushed against the side window. The box had large lettering which simply read *SKID*. Was I seeing things? I peered more closely. That's right, it read *SKID*. I turned back, gazing at the top window in the (now) brick house, at the room where Patrick had first taken me in his arms. I knew Pat was still there, trying to tell me something.

I recalled my first trip to Petworth when I was first discovering the existence of John and Katherine, and how when that memorable week was over, Patrick had popped into the picture; on the plane trip home, a man in front of me holding his newspaper up to show the headline, *Patrick White Dies*. Then there was the foxglove dream which I now realized was about healing; *"Heal, heal,"* the foxglove in Scotland seemed to say.

As the car with the SKID lettering pulled away from the curb, I knew what had to be done.

I phoned Dane (for years I'd noticed his ad in *Issues*, a local spiritual and holistic magazine), and made arrangements for a past life regression, or a current life regression, to get the root of the problem. I needed answers as to why Patrick White was still in my life, twenty years after his death. Maybe Dane could take me back to the 1970s, to the mess that Patrick and I had made of things.

Dane said he would come to my place the following week.

Konni phoned. I told her about my upcoming regression. "Good luck," she said, sarcastically. Konni was referring to a time when she had tried to communicate with Pat and he had challenged her, giving her a hard time. "Patrick is a spirit with an attitude," she had said.

Dane was a tall man in his sixties, and had an intriguing past. He was an ex-Catholic priest, who had turned to past life regressions as his new profession. "Why did you leave the Church?" I asked.

Dane smiled. "I left the Church when I realized that the God I served was within me and wasn't a separate entity."

Over a cup of tea, Dane asked if I had a particular area of interest for my regression.

"Patrick."

"Tell me about him."

I inhaled slowly. "Patrick was a young man I knew as a teen.

We went out for a while. I became pregnant and left town, and later we went our separate ways. Pat died at age twenty-three."

I didn't feel close enough to Dane to share with him Skid's wide wicked smile, his strong muscular arms, or his slow saunter. Instead, I kept to facts. "And we do seem to have unresolved business," I mumbled, shrugging my shoulders.

"All right," Dane said, reaching for his notebook, "let's see what we can do."

Dane sat in a chair with pen and paper, while I lay on the bed trying to relax.

After several post-hypnotic suggestions from Dane I began to feel as though I was slipping into another dimension, although I was still aware of noises outside the window.

"Where are you?" Dane asked.

I was vaguely aware of my surroundings, my body warm under the comforter, a distant train whistle, and yet I felt myself traveling through time and space.

"Where are you? " Dane asked again.

"At Patrick's grave." I could see the familiar cemetery that was high on a hill looking out to majestic Mt. Begbie.

"What are you wearing?" Dane asked.

The cemetery, wide and spacious, suddenly shrank. I twirled around. Patrick's grave was surrounded by tall, spindly trees, and the nearby graves had disappeared.

"What are you wearing?" Dane repeated.

I looked down in horror. I was wearing a pure white lacy dress liberally splattered with blood.

"What has happened?" Dane asked, his voice seemed distant.

I had stabbed myself. My body was sinking to the earthen grave, my blood soaking Patrick's gravesite.

Dane's voice cut through the scene. "Let's go back one month. What do you see?"

The bloody dress image vanished. Instead, my body burned

with humiliation. I couldn't tell Dane what I saw. I was no longer able to differentiate between Jewelle laying on the bed and the scene before me, and I couldn't understand that I was simultaneously existing in two realities.

"Where are you?" Dane asked.

"Germany."

"Where in Germany?"

"Black Forest."

"When?"

"1800s."

"What is your name?"

"Katarina."

"All right, Katarina, what do you see?"

I blurted, "I've just murdered my child!"

"How did this come about?" Dane asked gently.

"I've drowned my baby."

My body was cold and wet. I was shaking uncontrollably, although I lay on the bed under a warm comforter.

I was most distressed and repeated, "I've just given birth in water and I let my baby drown."

My God, I am so ashamed, so embarrassed. Dane must think me the most horrible, sinful woman.

"Look closer at the water," Dane said. *"Take your time. Slowly now. What do you see?"*

I lay in a small pool of water, tucked away in the woods; no one is with me. The water is murky with blood. An abortion! I've had a self-induced abortion!

"Look closer."

I had chosen water to abort, to hide the evidence. There was no child, only blood and tissue. Eventually, drained and exhausted, I leave the pool and return home.

"Katarina, are you married?"

"Yes."

"To Patrick?"

"No."

"Why did you abort your child?"

"Because my husband has been away a very long time and is to return home soon."

"Is he the father of the child?"

"No."

"Who is the father?"

"Patrick."

"Do you love your husband?"

"No."

"Do you love Patrick?"

"Yes"

"You could not be with him?"

"No."

"Why?"

"My husband would kill him."

"What happens?"

"I have the abortion and go home."

"Then what happens?"

"Patrick dies in an accident. I couldn't bear it. I go to his fresh grave dressed in a white dress to symbolize true love. I stab myself, my blood soaks the ground, the blood from my body mingling with Patrick's body deep in his grave."

"Leave Germany behind and in its place, send warm loving energy washing over the situation." Dane paused. *"Are there any other lives where you and Patrick have loved and lost?"*

It was like turning a TV channel. There was Wales, green and rugged, in the 1700s. One scene told the story.

"Patrick's blue eyes were dark with fury. We had been lovers, we had quarrelled. I'll show him, I thought, and I'd married another. And he showed me. He left on a ship bound for the New World, never to return."

197

"What else do you see in your Welsh life?"

I could see nothing.

"Are there any other lives where you and Patrick have loved and lost?"

"Many, many times we have repeated this same scenario, with various backgrounds."

"I'm going to bring Patrick into the room with us," Dane explained, "and you can talk with him."

Dane's suggestion would have surprised me, except for the altered state in which I floated.

"Babe," Patrick drawled.

"Hi, Skid." I felt shy. Patrick only slightly resembled the young man that I had known. Patrick had aged along with me and he was showing me how he looked, had he lived. Patrick's face was now slightly weathered, a tan accenting his deep blue eyes, and his whole being resonated with wisdom and love.

We walked hand in hand and our souls connected with love, only love. Then he dropped my hand, and in each of his hands he held two garbage bags.

"I'm taking these with me, Babe. I'll drop them off somewhere." As if he were hailing a cab, a pink hot air balloon, with an attached basket, appeared. Patrick plopped the bags into the basket. Seconds before the balloon lifted, with Patrick aboard, I began laughing.

"Pat, I get it! I understand! These bags are our garbage!"

"Garbage to be let go of, Jewelle. Next time we'll do it right." And as the balloon rose, Patrick was smiling that wicked Irish smile.

I slowly opened my eyes to see Dane finishing up his notes. Patrick died in 1974; it was now 1997. Our souls had finally begun to heal.

Twenty-seven

The calm, almost euphoric, feelings that enveloped me at the end of my regression with Patrick remained long after the experience ended. Patrick and I were healed. Man, this felt good!

My emotions, which had been trapped all those years by his death, broke free. Now I was happy to speak about him, to remember him.

As I poured coffee for local customers, I would ask, "Do you remember Patrick White—Skid?" And, of course, everyone remembered Pat; he was "that kind of a guy." I began asking Patrick's peers for their memories.

Dale Davis laughed as he remembered the party nights.

Ron Lind still had a vision of Skid's persona as *Mr. Tough-guy*, and yet a perfect gentleman with the girls. Ron, like Dale, had the party memories. "But you know," Ron said, "what stands out the most for me was that Patrick was a genuine guy who played no games."

Gordie Olsson recalled a nonchalant Patrick, who had not a care in the world.

"At least, not on the outside," I said.

"Yeah," Gordie agreed, "not on the outside."

Sunday mornings at the restaurant were busy, leaving no

time to chit chat with customers. I had been assigned to a section, and presumably would take little notice of the rest of the restaurant. I was taking an order, I remember, when he walked in the door. I watched the hostess take him to another section. A Patrick lookalike - a handsome young man, yet strangely, his clothes were old fashioned, from the 60s. Not retro-sixties, just outdated clothes, as if he'd come through a time warp.

There was a lull at my tables, and I found an excuse to walk through the section where "Patrick" was sitting. Our eyes met, probably because I was staring at him. Later, when I returned once again to check out the young old-fashioned man, he had left the restaurant.

I needed to get even closer to Pat, and thought of his best friend. The phone call to Ron Beraducci, Skid's old buddy, was heartwarming. Behind Ron's male bravado and deep laugh was his affection for his friend. Ron spoke with an honest and teasing manner about Pat, as if he were in the same room.

"Patrick and I met in grade school," Ron began. "Did you know that Pat had intended on becoming a Roman Catholic priest?"

"No way!" I was shocked.

"Yes. He and I both attended a Catholic school in Edmonton. The priesthood never happened, but for a while that was Pat's goal."

Ron laughed. "In later years, this is what would really piss off Pat. We'd be at a party and I'd call him *Father Patrick*. He would glare like hell, probably afraid it would ruin his image."

"Hey, his *Mr. Cool* image worked with me," I said. "To me, he was James Dean."

"That was all show," Ron said. "He put on an act; inside he was a pussycat. Once, a bunch of us guys went to Vancouver, and we were at a party. We all decided to leave, except Skid who said he'd meet us later. The next morning he came hobbling in with a fat lip, bruises, and practically needed crutches."

Ron was enjoying his old memories as he repeated, "It was all a show. As long as Patrick had his safety net of Revelstoke, he was okay. If he had lived, Pat would never have left Revelstoke."

"So, you're saying that Pat was insecure?"

Ron's voice became serious. "Sure Pat was insecure. He had lost his older brother, Michael—his only rock, his hero."

This was a whole side to Pat that I hadn't known or even recognized, but at age 17, all I saw was the surface Patrick.

After hanging up the phone, I was happy to know that Pat had had good friends who still loved him and who were happy to share their memories of him.

My own motives for talking about Pat were becoming clear to me. I wanted to write about Skid, to bring him back to life, if only on the pages in a book. A voice inside me asked what Patrick would think of that.

The clock on the wall indicated I had half an hour before my restaurant shift began. Hastily I ironed my uniform, dressed, and drove to the cemetery.

"Pat, we need to talk," I began, addressing the gray headstone. "I would like to write about you, but I need your permission." All was quiet, a breeze was all I felt.

"Pat, please, just give me a sign, one way or the other." Nothing.

"What do you expect," I chastised myself, "a bolt of lightening? You're standing in a cemetery, for Christ's sake, trying to speak with the dead!"

I looked at my watch. It was time for work. I walked back to my car, kicking a stone. As I opened the car door, a thought blazed in my head. *'If you hear "Crazy Love," then you know to write about me.'*

Crazy Love, by Van Morrision, the song, for me, which brings Patrick right to my side.

"And how long do I wait to hear this song?" I challenged the voice. "A month, a year?"

'This is crazy,' I thought, 'not *Crazy Love*. *Crazy Jewelle* is more like it!'

The restaurant was packed. The kitchen wheel was full of orders. The dim hum of voices and a ringing cash register created an atmosphere of urgency. I smiled a "hello" to "Mrs. Bridges." I put on my apron and took an order at a table. A tourist asked how many miles it was to Calgary. Another customer asked for directions to the enormous Revelstoke Dam.

Then I heard it. Barely audible over the restaurant's dull roar was Van Morrison's haunting voice. *Crazy Love*. I looked at the clock. Twenty minutes had passed since I stood beside Patrick's grave, asking for a sign. Through blurred vision, I clipped an order to the wheel. Kathy stared at me. I gave her a weak smile. "I'll explain later."

Later, I wondered if this was merely a coincidence, hearing "Crazy Love" only minutes after receiving the thought in my head. However, as I write these words, five years have passed since that day, and although I constantly listen to the radio, "Crazy Love" has never played for me again.

As Cindy snipped and styled my hair, I enjoyed, as always, her quips of spiritual wisdom. I asked Cindy, "What's new?"

"I'm going to Banff this weekend for a *Kryon* Seminar."

"What's *Kryon*?"

"*Kryon* is channeled material from an energy here to help the planet in its transformation into the next times; it's an energy that's realigning the grid system, to help us understand and heal what's happening on our planet. Volcanoes, hurricanes, and floods are all signs that Mother Nature is rebelling. That's my interpretation of *Kryon*," Cindy said.

"And who is the channel of *Kryon*?"

"Lee Carroll. He and Jan Tober are the facilitators of the *Kryon* seminars."

After a moment of silence, Cindy asked, "And what's new with you?"

I told Cindy about my need to write again, but didn't mention my recent experiences with Pat. Instead, I mused, "You know, my direction when I was in Britain was so clear, to come back to Revelstoke, but now that I'm here the path isn't always clear and . . ."

Cindy interrupted, "The *mothership!*"

"What?"

"England is your mothership, your soul's home, where you get further instructions on the next leg of your life's journey," Cindy crowed triumphantly.

I had to digest this as Cindy put the finishing touches on my hair.

"Cindy Powell. I knew your name was familiar when I first met you. It was John Lennon's first wife's name."

We laughed in delight at the coincidence and then, wishing Cindy a good weekend with *Kryon*, I waved her a fond farewell.

Work at the restaurant was getting to me. My chest hurt constantly from breathing the ever-present blue smoke. I felt trapped. The *Catch 22* was that I needed a new job, but I was too tired to look for another one.

Years later I would hear Oprah say, "Do what you love and the money will follow." My love was for my story of John and Katherine, or did I just simply love John? For a while my book had been my passion, but I'd never given the story the *all* that it deserved, and eventually I'd given up. I'd nearly forgotten that Revelstoke was supposed to be a classroom in the school of my life.

One night, after work, I sat in my apartment and did my weekly budget, taking a scrap of paper out of a junk drawer to juggle my money numbers. Writing, on the reverse side of the paper caught my eye. *"If we can discover our past and its relevance to today, then we can be rest assured of our future. If we have evidence that our souls are an endless entity, residing in a temporary body, then it should be obvious that our home is an infinite Universe, a playground of limitless learning."*

I recognized my handwriting, and vaguely remembered writing these thoughts in a time when I was in a different head space. I knew my approach to life these days was all wrong, and there was probably a cosmic reason for putting on my waitress' uniform each day.

The next afternoon, I listlessly ironed my white blouse for yet another working day when the phone rang. The call display said "California," although it wasn't Konni's number.

A woman's voice said, "Hello, this is Jan Tober. I'm trying to locate Jewelle Lewis."

"Yes, that's me."

"Wonderful," her cheerful voice continued, "I'm calling about your book, *Just Imagine.*"

"Jan Tober, Jan Tober," my mind raced, the name familiar.

"Lee Carroll and I just held a *Kryon* seminar in Banff and while there, I discovered your book. A friend of yours has *insisted* that I call you."

I recalled my conversation with Cindy. Did Cindy insist that Jan Tober call me?

"Cindy asked you to call me?" I asked.

"Cindy? Ah, no. Your friend, John, asked me to call you."

"John?" I asked, confused.

"John Lennon," Jan said.

"John Lennon asked you to call me?" I repeated, later thinking I must have sounded like a total dunce.

"Yes," Jan explained, "I've worked with John's spirit for a very long time. Your book jumped out at me, and it was like he was pushing me to pick it up."

Tears burned my eyes. I knew this conversation was important.

"Honey," Jan said, "John thanks you for telling your story; his and your story. Jewelle, John has asked me to sing for you."

Jan's voice was light and beautiful as she sang for me, from California, an Irish ballad, *Black is the Colour*, and I accepted with all my soul the love that poured through the phone lines.

As if the flood gates of the Revelstoke Dam had opened, I spilled with emotion. "Jan, I had begun to believe that John had forgotten me." My thoughts and words were disjointed. "My book has been out for a while, but it's all on hold it seems. I have personal stuff to deal with. Maybe I'm hiding here in the mountains. I just feel so alone with this story."

"Honey, John has not left you, he's just waiting, standing back, letting you sort things out."

Becky's English voice came to mind, as she, too, had conveyed John's message. *"Follow your heart Katherine. I am here waiting in the wings."*

If I'd known, at the time of Jan's first call, the extent of her involvement in the planet's spiritual development, I may have been too humbled and shy to carry on a conversation with this beautiful and enlightened lady. As time passed, I learned of Jan Tober's and Lee Carroll's widely known Kryon seminars and Kryon channeled books. The title of their book, "Indigo Children," is now a household word. Jan and Lee have spoken to people around the world, including the United Nations. In Jan's younger career days, she was a jazz musician with such mentors and employers as Fred Astaire, Stan Keaton, and the "King of Swing," Benny Goodman. Recently, Jan released a CD, "Teknicolor Tapestry," in which she thanked many musicians, including her spiritual friend, John Lennon.

A realization, and an awakening, pounded in my head. *"Jan Tober called you with a message from the spirit of John Lennon. The message is real. All of it has always been real. You just needed validation, and you got it. Now go with it. Do what you're supposed to do with your life!"*

Twenty-eight

J an Tober's (and John's) call was a sweet, magical moment, giving me the energy and enthusiasm to leave the restaurant and forge ahead. My school classes in Revelstoke were over, it seemed. After all, Patrick and I had healed. Wasting not one moment, I phoned the restaurant, giving my two week's notice. Hanging up the phone, I felt light and free. I wondered where I should start my new life. Three seconds later, my phone rang.

The lady on the line got right to the point. "I'm opening a private home for senior citizens and I need a house mother. You could live right in the house and work a shift as well."

"Are you offering me a job?" I asked, laughing.

"Yes."

"Great, I'll take it!"

"You will?"

"Yes, when do I start?"

I knew the timing of the job offer, arriving seconds after my decision to leave town, meant only one thing. My time here was not quite finished.

The House, as I called my new home and workplace, sat inconspicuously on a near-downtown street. The interior of the house, however, was breathtaking, and I gasped when I first entered the home that reminded me of a manor house from days gone by. *The House* shone. Fresh flowers adorned polished furniture and gourmet meals created by fabulous cooks made *The House* a home.

Willy, short for Wilma, was the first resident to move in. Charismatic and outspoken, Willy managed to keep the staff, including me, on our toes. Blunt, yet lovable, that was Willy.

Louise moved in the next day. I was shocked. I hadn't seen Mrs. DeBlass since she helped deliver my baby, three decades ago. Instantly, a memory emerged. My baby had just been born, but before I could see him, another nurse whisked him away. As I raised my head, all I could see was a tiny purple foot emerging from a white blanket. In the moments that followed I would have lost my mind, I'm sure, if not for the nurse, Louise DeBlass, her kind words easing the most difficult moment of my life.

The gentle retired nurse didn't recognize me, but I knew that the Universe had provided me with an opportunity to return some of the care and kindness that she had once given me.

As Willy became more comfortable in her new surroundings, she began reminiscing of days gone by. Willy began talking about Patrick White. I was stunned.

"You knew Patrick?" I asked.

"Knew him? I lived next door to him and watched him grow up."

For the next two years it always amazed me, listening to Willy's neighborhood stories that included Patrick.

Mrs. DeBlass was failing rapidly and she needed more care than we could provide. The morning she was to leave, Louise sat patiently on her bed waiting for her ride. I ran up the stairs and knocked on her door. I blurted breathlessly, "Mrs. DeBlass, I must speak with you before you leave."

"Yes, dear?" she looked at me kindly.

"I know you don't remember me, but in 1970 I had a baby

and you helped deliver him. I was a teenager . . . I want to thank you; you were very kind to me and I never forgot you."

The frail lady smiled sadly. "There were so many girls . . ."

A knock on the door announced Louise's ride and her departure from my life.

All aspects of my life were wrapped up in the world of the seniors home, and most of my contact with the outside world was via phone. *The House*, a bustling entity by day was, by nine at night, silent, a time when I wondered why I was here and how did I get here?

Konni and I spoke often by phone, but no longer about psychic matters. My sister's MS had consumed her body, and the recent loss of her teenage son, Layne, had stolen her spirit. Thank God for Larry, Konni's husband, whose care was based on *All You Need Is Love*, for better or for worse.

One night, Moira called. Would I like to come and visit her? Did I get a day off? No, I never got a full day off, but I did get *hours* off. It was arranged that the next Sunday we would spend the day together.

Only when I travelled the misty valleys, leaving Revelstoke, did I realize how little time I spent away from *The House*.

Moira was happy that I'd arrived in time to attend church with her. "Church?" I asked, surprised.

"A spiritual church," she said.

I had heard of spiritual churches in England, but I didn't know we had them in Canada, let alone so close to home.

The congregation consisted of about thirty members and as we prayed and sang hymns, it seemed the same as any other church service. That is, until the minister stood before us with messages from departed loved ones. The mood changed; there was electricity in the air. As the minister called on various members, I noticed that the messages were personal to the ones receiving them and were all from departed family.

The minister called out yet another name. *"Jewelle."*

I jumped. For me? A message for me? As I was a guest, I didn't expect to be included in this way.

"I have a man here; he is not of your family, but he loves you very much."

"Patrick?" Moira mouthed silently. I shrugged my shoulders as the minister continued.

"Jewelle, a few years ago, your spirit nearly brought your life to a halt."

How could I forget when my soul had asked to slip away? I nodded my head as the minister continued.

"The man here with you today sends his love, and to confirm his identity for you he wants to describe his death. The man wants to assure you that he is now all right, but at the time of his passing he was fatally wounded in his shoulder and back area; the blow's impact had actually spun him around. He wants you to know that he's smiling and he has no more pain."

The minister had moved on to another person as I sat in stunned silence absorbing the simplistic, yet accurate, message. The minister didn't say *why* my life nearly came to an end, only that it nearly did, which was correct. More importantly to me, the minister had just described John Lennon's death, relaying the message, without knowing the identity of the messenger. Once again I could hear John's words, through Becky, *"It's me again, just a different channel."*

After church Moira and I had a leisurely lunch, and passed the afternoon talking about our mutual love—England. Moira has traveled across the pond often, and we laughed as we compared our accumulated air miles.

Then, like Cinderella, I realized my time had slipped by and I would have to hurry back to *The House*.

"Before you go," said Moira, "let's light a candle for Patrick."

Moira lit a white candle and, as we sat in silence, Patrick's spirit came close enabling us to feel his presence.

"Patrick is at peace," Moira began. *"He's been waiting to tell you, ever since your regression, that he knows you loved him as he loved you. Words, that as teens, neither of you expressed."*

Tears flowed down my face, and I looked at Moira whose own cheeks were damp. We laughed because we had cried, and the candle's flame seemed to dance with joy.

"Yes, I loved Patrick White and I know that he loved me. For decades I denied this love because of the pain it brought, yet I've been in pain all along. Until my regression, that is, when we walked hand in hand."

"And that," Moira stated, "is what Patrick wants to say; he's happy and at peace, now that you both have finally expressed your love for each other. Simple as that."

The new millennium was approaching, but in my world it may as well have been the turn of the seventeenth or eighteenth century. I had taken to wearing long black skirts, and often imagined my hair done up in a bun. One day while taking a tray to an ill lady's room I felt something lightly touch my back, and I had a vision of myself wearing a servant's cap with white ribbons cascading down my back. Willy commented on how I seemed to be made for this job. "It fits you to a tee," she would say.

I began to view *The House* as a medieval or even a Victorian household. The hallways and archways, the kitchen and housekeeping staff, could easily have been part of a regimented house from whatever century you chose. Even a panel of lights on my bedroom wall was a modern version of the bell system, used for centuries, connecting the residents of the house to the servants' quarters. With one new resident, a cranky and mean woman, I was often tempted to curtsey and say, "Yes, ma'am," but following the rules set out for any hired help, I bit my tongue and smiled instead!

One afternoon, I escaped *The House* for the solitude of the public library. A children's display of books caught my eye, as did a book about girls in Medieval times. Thumbing through the pages, I was stunned when one sentence jumped out. *In Medieval times, girls were commonly taught the skills of nursing.* I understood exactly. The book didn't mean modern nursing, where today's nurses know nearly as much as doctors. No, medieval nursing meant caring for the sick, the poor, and the homeless. Medieval nursing described exactly my role in *The House*, or caring for Audrey, and even home healthcare. *Or Katherine caring for John.*

"Oh, my God," I whispered, replacing the book in the display. I recalled Dayle's words, once written in a letter. "*Our lives are a pattern, a tapestry for us to recognize, and to unravel the design.*"

I now understood why Marie, Audrey's niece, had commented, "I can just see you doing homecare hundreds of years ago, bustling about in a long, black skirt, with your hair in a bun."

Clearly I could see the pattern of my current life that paralleled Katherine's role in the ancient hospital, and I was dumb founded to realize I had not seen the connection before today. Not only had my grief over John been stuck in time, but other aspects of my past as Katherine also remained, destined to repeat itself this time around. At age 17 working in a house, to caring for Audrey, to homecare, and to working and living in The House, was a pattern, a major design in the tapestry of my past and current life.

I phoned Therese Dorer, a recommended channeler from Kamloops, a lady who didn't know me or my story, and made an appointment for a reading to be done by phone. Any spiritual contact from John would be appreciated.

Twenty-nine

A week later Therese and I connected by phone, and she began by asking if I still wanted a reading.

"Why?" I asked, confused.

Therese explained, "After we set up our appointment I recognized your name, and realized I'd read your book, *Just Imagine*. I know you wanted a reading by someone who knows nothing about you."

I did a quick assessment. "Therese," I said, "your honesty says it all. Please, let's do the reading."

Therese took a deep breath and, after a prayer, she began. *"Jewelle, I have with you a beautiful lady, dressed in a shimmering white dress. She says, 'Congratulations for your courage and for searching and telling your story.' Although you are feeling displaced at the moment, she asks that you have faith and trust that you will be guided towards a successful conclusion. Yes, the last steps have been rocky and will continue to be quite a climb, but you will reach the mountain top."*

Therese said, "I'm asking this lovely spirit lady, what was the purpose of Jewelle following this path?"

"The lady says, 'There needs to be closure between these two souls, Katherine and John, who were so closely connected.' "

Therese paused, then announced, "John has just popped in."

I laughed. "I knew he would!"

Therese continued, *"John's showing me two sides of himself. One side is the John I recognize, Beatle John. He stands by a gate, an entrance to a meadow. He has an open book and he puts his hands on the pages and says, 'The new book will be written.' I now see the other side of John, an old fashioned John. He wears a waistcoat, he's on a hill; it's windy, and he's holding a bouquet of purple wildflowers for you. John is showing us a huge clock, and he's saying, 'There is no time.' He walks now and wants us to come with him. He shows us a big stone house and says, 'Wealth and materialism do not serve us. We will walk the earth many times, learning all of our lessons.'"*

Therese paused as the scene before her changed. *"John is showing me where he is comfortable; a stone bench, a tree, it's Spring. John thanks you for being on this side of the veil. He knows there are many who don't understand where you are. So many circumstances have taken your energy, he knows, but remember there is work to be done here on earth. Have patience and trust in your destiny. Just flow . . . the energy will see you through."*

"May I speak to John myself?" I asked.

"Yes, certainly," Therese said.

"John, hello. Are you happy? Are you okay?"

"Yes, yes," he answered through Therese. *"I am in a very enlightened place. I am in a circle of energy, a pure crystalline light, and a beautiful place. I have so many masters; we in spirit can affect change on earth and will affect change."*

Therese said, "John is giving me a message. Please bear with me as I try to relay the words. *John says to all, 'Trust and believe in love. Love is really all there is, that is, all there is, is love.'"*

I interrupted, "Does John mean, all you need is love?"

Therese burst out laughing. "Oh, my God, of course! I forgot I was talking with John Lennon!" After a good chuckle, Therese said there was more to relay.

"I'm getting the sense that John, in spirit, is working here on earth. He's showing me an artist's palette and he says, 'The consciousness of the planet can be raised through the arts.' Now, it's the old-fashioned John speaking. He says to you, 'I will always be around for you, but I also have work to do outside of the earth's realm.' "

Therese asked, "Is there any parting message that you have for John?"

"I love you, John Baron."

Therese's voice was soft, *"When you say that, it takes him right back to the English countryside, and he sends you his love. John says to you, 'We will meet in the afterlife; there will be a grand reunion.' "*

The phone rang. It was 6:00 a.m., and it was my mother's voice. Konni had died. My blood turned to ice. *Konni was gone, passed away in her sleep with no warning and no goodbyes.* I carried out my work duties until about noon, when the shock wore off, and I broke down. *How can I live without my sister?* My mourning was shared with family from British Columbia to California. Konni had been a wife, a mother, a daughter, a sister, a cousin, an aunt, and a niece, the minister said. *Konni had also been a friend, I thought—my best friend.*

Konni's funeral was held on a beautiful September afternoon and our family gathered in a little church on the beach of the Shuswap Lake. Konni had been christened in this church forty-three years earlier. Konni had grown up and left Canada, taking Larry and the United States into her heart. Now she returned home; her life had come full circle.

The weeks following Konni's death were still and quiet. My call display no longer announced calls from California, but in my mind I can still capture my sister's voice. She would laugh to know I've written this, but I now savor the sound.

I've tried to recall how my first experience with channeling came about, but the memory is vague. I do remember sitting, with a pen and a piece of paper, and writing, "Konni, I don't feel I have anything to say, to write about. If there's something that you'd like to say, feel free to use this pen . . ." The pen suddenly felt light and airy in my hand and, with two minutes, the following words appeared.

"Tell the story, Jewelle, of your past life, which is not even the past; it's all now, it's all one life. We think our lives are separate; it's all one play, one picture. Tell of your English life and how it's part of you now. That's why it's part of you now, because nothing ends. You take your clothes off at night, but you're still there. Later your body dies, but your soul is still there—just changing elements, body to body, which has nothing to do with your soul—it's never ending. Tell your story so others can see where their lives are; what is their big picture, for the big picture is the only picture. A piece of the puzzle does not stand alone; it's part of the whole picture. That is what departed souls are trying to tell people on earth. You should see all the souls—imagine all the people (Konni smiles at her joke.) *For here we are still people; nothing has changed. You should see all the people trying to communicate with those ones that they love. It's so simple. We're not parted any more than when a child goes to school and returns at night. We are all in different schools. This is not heaven, where I am. There is no heaven, no hell, just another classroom."*

    Love,
    Konni

I stared at the paper, feeling Konni's presence and it felt so natural. I remembered how, for years, I had wanted to communicate with John, but I lacked confidence in my abilities, so I rarely tried. Communicating with Konni, however, was easy. After all, we'd been doing it our whole lives. Much of our conversation over the past decade had been of the spirit world, and now that Konni was there herself, death didn't seem to me to be so much of a mystery. I read Konni's channeled words as if she were sending me a postcard from a foreign land, a place to where we would all eventually travel.

I re-read Konni's words. If I looked at my story from a different angle, viewing the past and present as one big production, it all made sense, sort of. John had said it himself, through channeling from Judy. *"Our deepest feelings are still felt, these three hundred years, because the soul is able to see all."*

"Yes, yes!" I was becoming excited as pieces of the mystery began falling into place.

I grabbed a copy of *Just Imagine*, and read the words that John had channeled describing Katherine's and John's life. This was not the Petworth life, but another lifetime of theirs. I was beginning to understand how we probably live and re-live in such a similar manner that our lives are difficult to differentiate, one from another.

The message from John, relayed through Judy, was a decade old and only now it was becoming clear. Judy had asked John, *"Tell me the story of John and Jewelle."*

"Once upon a time . . . just kidding! Okay, our lives mostly take place in the south of England. Southeast, actually. We were young and truly wild for each other. Our marriage was one of beauty. We were very sociable, with many people to see and important functions to attend. Yes, Katherine and Jewelle are the same, as I am John Baron, or actually it was John the Baron, of York descent."

Judy asked, *"Can you describe Katherine and John?"*

"First, Katherine. Long auburn hair, she kept it tied back, and usually wore a hat or bonnet. She loved the color blue, and she could often be seen, from a distance, picking handfuls of flowers to put around the kitchen. Mother thought maybe she was a little light-headed, but I never told her. She was sensitive and easily hurt by the words of others. We enjoyed the fire and hot, fresh breads.

"John is a man of considerable height, over six feet, I would say. I will visit them later. For now, I will say he was of a spiritual nature. He believed in prayer and honesty and truth for all. Perhaps this was his downfall, for he was naive in his belief in others that eventually cost him. But to describe him—he had a good lot of hair and a very pronounced face with a large jaw. The pain of parting was great, really, as it wasn't time for us to part, but we had to accept it despite our frustration."

Over a space of ten years, since first receiving Judy's channeling, until Konni's words from the spirit world, I hadn't understood what *"I will visit them later"* meant. John had recently shown Therese a huge clock and had said, *"There is no time,"* and Konni had said, *"Our lives are all one play."* This new concept was beginning to make sense to my human brain, and I realized that we don't have to completely understand something to believe it's real.

Thirty

Dreams came quickly that night, as my subconscious mind sorted through the events of the day.

A radio newscaster was announcing Patrick's sudden death when the broadcast changed to the shocking news of John Lennon's death. My dream became the dance at the Great Hall. John held Katherine in his arms, but when they spun around Katherine noticed that Patrick had replaced John. The fiddlers' music became rock and roll, while Katherine's rich green gown transformed into a white mini dress. The dream changed again. Rain and gray clouds were all Katherine could see from the narrow attic window. She knew there was no point trying the door, for it would be locked, as usual. Jewelle, as well, felt danger in the unwed mothers' home but, unlike Katherine, she was able to bolt out the door. The dream became present day in The House. The residents were away and, ghost-like, I floated through the empty rooms searching for John. The House disappeared, and I was flying over the South Downs in Sussex scouring the countryside, and finally I settled above the valley and waited.

I was still waiting when morning arrived.

Cindy called; would I like a walk this afternoon? Cindy's

mind is refreshingly open and, as we walked on Revelstoke's greenbelt, I felt free to share my dreams of last night with her.

"Jewelle, you've been searching for John your whole life."

"I have?"

"Your dream says it all. Patrick's death is John's death. The dance in the Seventies is the seventeenth century dance. Katherine's horrific last days are carried over to feelings of danger in the unwed mothers' home. You've been searching for John ever since he was taken away, to God knows where, never to return."

Cindy looked at me thoughtfully. "Where do you spend most of your time in England?"

"Overlooking the valley," I replied.

"You've probably lost count of your trips to Petworth. Could you financially afford any of those flights?"

"Not one," I said.

"Just to overlook a valley," Cindy stated gently.

"You're too clever," I smiled.

We walked in silence for a while before Cindy blurted, "Life is a set-up!"

"A set-up?"

"Sure. We write our life script before we are born, and later we're amazed when the right people and circumstances enter our lives when, really, we've arranged it all ourselves."

I pondered Cindy's words for a while before the light bulb came on. "So I set up a life now to resemble my past life, enabling me to live through the grief and trauma that, in John's and Katherine's time, was impossible to do because their own lives were cut short. That explains the resemblance between my life with Patrick and my life with John; so I could heal this time around."

Talk about a set-up! I just happened to have a mother, a sister, a daughter, and a cousin who had their own special abilities and insight into the spirit world. They individually assisted me on my journey to discover the past and how it affected my present life.

When I first started searching, trying to prove just to myself whether I had known John in ancient England, my only expectation had been whether I could locate the records of names, places, and dates relating to our former selves. That was all. I never imagined that John would guide me and, in retrospect, I see that without his participation, my whole search would have ended long ago.

Cindy added, "John Lennon is *the* major player in your set-up. If John Baron had been John Doe in this life, instead of reincarnating as John Lennon, there would have been no trigger (your unexplained grief lasting for years) to begin your search. You and John probably wrote the script together."

I was ashamed, so very ashamed. I had never given John the acknowledgment he deserved. John had provided me with messages and coincidences (more than I've mentioned) that were so blatantly obvious as to his presence, and I would say, "That's nice," and wait for yet another sign. One day, I would believe. The next day, I doubted. My soul always knew John Baron and John Lennon were the same soul, but the modern, doubting, cynical me kept waiting for the ultimate sign to verify this.

"Cindy, even after writing a book about our story, I still often doubted the whole experience. Man, I can't stand people like me," I laughed bitterly.

"Hey, girl," Cindy put her arm around me, "don't be so down on yourself. Anyone in your situation would feel pulled between two worlds. Give yourself *some* credit for coming this far."

"With John Lennon," I stated with conviction.

"Yes, with John Lennon," Cindy smiled broadly.

When I viewed my past and present lives as a script in one giant play, the whole pattern was obvious. My father had once said to me, *"Jewelle, you can't re-live your past life."* Well, I have been doing just that, and you, dear reader, probably are too.

I've realized that our relationships across the centuries are like those wooden Russian dolls; one fits neatly inside the other and so on and so on. Sure, I lived an era with Patrick that resembled life with John yet, simultaneously, Patrick and I were working out issues from Germany and Wales. Again, I could visualize a hundred wooden dolls that all fit together, becoming one doll.

My patterns were giving me a headache, especially the realization that caregiving and living in residential/institutional-type houses was another deja vu. However, I didn't intend to investigate the reasons behind my repeated employment situation. *The House* had become overwhelmingly medieval to me, and that's all I needed to know.

I was tired of living in another century. I wanted a life in the new century. I wanted to look forward, not backward.

All You Need Is Love had given me the endurance needed for my twenty-year search. I loved Patrick, and my love for John Baron knows no bounds, but to investigate other tangents seems a waste of energy.

Some final loose ends began to come together. I read in a spiritual magazine about the ways spirits will try to reach us. Roses! The scent of roses means love from spirits, and I remembered my trip on the plane and in the taxi; the beautiful scent of roses followed me to Petworth. Or perhaps the rose scent was the white rose, the Baron family rose?

My thoughts turned to lavender and, after some quick research, I learned that lavender was often burned in sick rooms to sweeten and disinfect the air. My two-month cough after inhaling the scent was probably a past life memory of caring for the sick, I decided. The lavender scent had also evoked the haunting memory of an empty baby's cradle, and I wondered if this was a symbol of losing children.

The House became like a restrictive prison for me and, if I stayed, the ancient memories would mold me, I felt, into an uptight matron like Agnes from Katherine's day. *Been there, done that*, I was sure. I am grateful to the Universe for bringing Louise DeBlass and Willy Sjodin into my life via *The House*, but it was now time to go forward. My life classes in Revelstoke were over. I was healed.

Dayle, my cousin, says, *"Ask the Universe any question and you shall receive an answer."* All I wanted was one little answer. Thick, wet snowflakes fell while I was driving to the post office for my mail. As I drove, I looked skyward and pleaded with the white Universe, "Please tell me what I'm supposed to be doing with my life. Please give me a sign, any sign."

I retrieved my mail and returned to my car. Glancing through the pile of bills, I noticed an envelope with the return name and address of Jan Tober. I reviewed my call from Jan that momentous day. I recalled my reaction, a reaction I had forgotten all about, just like I'd let the importance of her words slip into the recesses of my brain. How could I have just forgotten Jan's call?

As I started to open her card, I had the same realization that I'd had the day of Jan's call. Those thoughts pounded in my head this snowy afternoon, as they had long ago. *Jan Tober called you with a message from the spirit of John Lennon. The message is real. All of it has always been real. You just needed validation and you got it. Now go with it. Do what you're supposed to do with your life!*

In my excitement to open the envelope, I'd jerked the card. Instantly, there were bits of gold flying through my car. Gold angels—hundreds, it seemed, of tiny, sparkling golden angels! I laughed and I cried. The sign, I had requested moments earlier, had been given. Jan's golden angels reminded me of what I'd known for a long time. My life's purpose is to tell my past life story.

In October, 2001, I took Joanne to Petworth. Joanne said it was like visiting her mother's homeland. Or the *mothership*, as Cindy would say. We visited the tourist spots from London to York, but the best time was being with Ros and Ann, and their families and friends. I did spend time alone, overlooking the valley and wandering the lanes of Petworth.

I saw the strangest sight in the window of a secondhand bookstore—a large book rack with only two books on display. One book was titled, *Baron's Ballet* and the other, *The Beatles*. It was eerie to see the two titles, as if John Baron and John Lennon had come together on a book rack in Petworth.

The flight home was the toughest departure of any visit to Petworth so far. As the plane ascended, I strained to watch out the aircraft window, through bits of mist and clouds, to the green rolling countryside.

When England vanished from sight, I burst into tears.

Two weeks after arriving home from England, a letter arrived from Ros. She had enclosed an article from Petworth's newspaper, *The Midhurst and Petworth Observer*. I was stunned beyond words, as I read.

"Artwork by the late John Lennon has gone on show in Petworth this week. In a coup for the historic market town, a collection of 130 sketches and drawings by the former Beatle has been loaned to the Saddler Row Gallery. The show includes nine drawings, from Yoko Ono's own private collection, that have never been seen in public before."

I quickly scanned the article and one sentence jumped out at me.

"We are pleased that we managed to get it for Petworth, as it is only being displayed in four galleries in the UK . . ."

Four? Only *four* galleries were chosen in all of the United

Kingdom for John's art show. **Petworth** was chosen from thousands of towns and major cities in Britain? Petworth would display John Lennon's art for thirteen days in November, 2001.

John, like Katherine, had returned home.

Jewelle St. James, today
(PHOTO: VINCENT WRIGHT)

To visit our website:
www.pastlifewithjohnlennon.com